GOVTIKTALK

The 48 Laws of GSA Contracting

Author: Ramon Claiborne
Copyright © 2024 by @GovTikTalk

Published by Most Definite Publishing

ISBN: 9798883604798

Printed in United States of America

Contents

A note from the Author

Continuously innovate your products, services, and solutions to stay relevant and competitive within the GSA marketplace.

Law 8, Page 30
Deliver Exceptional Value
Strive to exceed client expectations by consistently delivering high-quality products and services under GSA contracts.

Law 9, Page 32
Protect Your Reputation
Guard your reputation and integrity fiercely, as they are crucial assets in the world of government contracting.

Law 10, Page 35
Communicate Effectively
Develop clear and concise communication strategies to convey your value proposition and differentiate yourself from competitors.

Law 11, Page 37
Leverage Information and Intelligence
Utilize market intelligence and data analytics to make informed decisions and gain a competitive edge.

Law 12, Page 40
Cultivate Patience and Persistence
Understand that success in GSA contracting often requires long-term dedication, patience, and persistence.

Law 13, Page 42
Manage Risk Prudently
Identify, assess, and mitigate risks associated with GSA contracts to protect your business interests and ensure compliance.

Law 14, Page 45
Foster Strategic Alliances

Form strategic partnerships and alliances with complementary firms to enhance your capabilities and broaden your reach within the GSA ecosystem.

Law 15, Page 48
Stay Informed and Adaptable
Keep abreast of changes in GSA regulations, policies, and procedures to adapt your strategies accordingly.

Law 16, Page 50
Think Long-Term
Adopt a long-term perspective in your approach to GSA contracting, focusing on building sustainable relationships and achieving enduring success.

Law 17, Page 53
Remain Vigilant Against Corruption
Maintain high ethical standards and vigilance against corruption or unethical practices that may jeopardize your business reputation or GSA contracts.

Law 18, Page 55
Be Mindful of Power Dynamics
Understand the power dynamics at play within the GSA environment and leverage them to your advantage ethically.

Law 19, Page 58
Foster a Culture of Excellence
Cultivate a culture of excellence and continuous improvement within your organization to excel in GSA contracting.

Law 20, Page 60
Adaptability over Rigidity
Be adaptable and willing to adjust your strategies and approaches based on evolving GSA requirements and market conditions.

Law 21, Page 63
Demonstrate Expertise and Authority

Establish yourself as a trusted authority and thought leader within your niche or industry segment to enhance your credibility and influence within the GSA marketplace.

Law 22, Page 66
Seize Opportunities Diligently
Identify and seize opportunities within the GSA Multiple Award Schedule promptly and diligently to gain a competitive advantage.

Law 23, Page 68
Exercise Discretion and Tact
Exercise discretion and tact in your interactions with GSA officials, clients, and competitors to maintain positive relationships and avoid unnecessary conflicts.

Law 24, Page 71
Cultivate Resilience
Develop resilience and perseverance to overcome setbacks, challenges, and rejections encountered in the GSA contracting process.

Law 25, Page 73
Invest in Continuous Learning
Commit to ongoing learning and professional development to stay ahead of the curve and adapt to the evolving landscape of GSA contracting.

Law 26, Page 76
Foster Transparency and Integrity
Maintain transparency in your dealings and adhere to high ethical standards to build trust and credibility with GSA and client stakeholders.

Law 27, Page 78
Strategically Manage Time and Resources
Effectively allocate time, manpower, and resources to maximize productivity and efficiency in pursuing and fulfilling GSA contracts.

Law 28, Page 81
Cultivate a Strong Brand Identity
Develop a strong brand identity and positioning to differentiate yourself and create a lasting impression in the minds of GSA clients and decision-makers.

Law 29, Page 84
Embrace Cultural Sensitivity and Diversity
Respect and embrace cultural diversity and sensitivity in your interactions with GSA officials, clients, and partners to foster inclusive and mutually beneficial relationships.

Law 30, Page 86
Stay Abreast of Compliance Requirements
Stay updated on regulatory and compliance requirements governing GSA contracts to ensure adherence and mitigate the risk of penalties or contract disputes.

Law 31, Page 89
Harness the Power of Data and Analytics
Leverage data analytics and business intelligence tools to gain actionable insights and inform strategic decision-making in pursuing and managing GSA contracts.

Law 32, Page 92
Emphasize Value Proposition Over Price
Focus on communicating the value and benefits of your offerings rather than solely competing on price to win GSA contracts and maintain profitability.

Law 33, Page 94
Develop a Robust Risk Management Framework
Establish a comprehensive risk management framework to identify, assess, mitigate, and monitor risks associated with GSA contracts proactively.

Law 34, Page 97

Cultivate a Culture of Compliance

Instill a culture of compliance and accountability within your organization to uphold GSA contract terms, regulations, and ethical standards rigorously.

Law 35, Page 99
Build Strategic Reserves and Contingencies

Maintain strategic reserves and contingencies to mitigate unforeseen risks, disruptions, and fluctuations in GSA contract demand or market conditions.

Law 36, Page 102
Exercise Diplomacy in Disputes and Conflicts

Approach disputes and conflicts with diplomacy, tact, and a commitment to finding mutually acceptable resolutions to preserve relationships and minimize disruptions to GSA contracts.

Law 37, Page 105
Continuously Evaluate and Improve Processes

Continuously evaluate and optimize your internal processes, workflows, and systems to streamline operations and enhance efficiency in managing GSA contracts.

Law 38, Page 108
Develop a Robust Competitive Intelligence Strategy

Invest in gathering and analyzing competitive intelligence to identify emerging trends, opportunities, and threats in the GSA marketplace and adjust your strategies accordingly

Law 39, Page 110
Anticipate and Adapt to Regulatory Changes

Anticipate and adapt to changes in GSA regulations, policies, and procurement practices to proactively position your organization for compliance and competitive advantage.

Law 40, Page 113
Foster a Customer-Centric Mindset

Prioritize customer satisfaction and responsiveness to client needs and feedback to cultivate strong, enduring relationships and secure repeat business under GSA contracts.

Law 41, Page 116
Invest in Talent Development and Retention
Invest in recruiting, training, and retaining top talent to build a skilled and motivated workforce capable of delivering exceptional performance on GSA contracts.

Law 42, Page 119
Pursue Strategic Growth Opportunities
Identify and pursue strategic growth opportunities, such as expanding into new GSA Schedule categories or target markets, to diversify revenue streams and mitigate risk.

Law 43, Page 122
Leverage Technology for Competitive Advantage
Embrace technology and innovation to gain a competitive edge in delivering innovative solutions and enhancing operational efficiency in fulfilling GSA contracts.

Law 44, Page 125
Foster Cross-Functional Collaboration
Foster collaboration and synergy across departments, teams, and stakeholders within your organization to optimize coordination and execution of GSA contract requirements.

Law 45, Page 128
Cultivate Flexibility and Adaptability
Cultivate a culture of flexibility and adaptability to respond swiftly and effectively to changing requirements, priorities, and opportunities within GSA contracts and the broader marketplace.

Law 46, Page 131
Demonstrate Commitment to Sustainability and Social Responsibility

Integrate sustainability and social responsibility initiatives into your business practices and GSA contract deliverables to align with evolving client expectations and regulatory trends.

Law 47, Page 134
Manage Stakeholder Expectations Effectively
Proactively manage stakeholder expectations, including those of GSA officials, clients, subcontractors, and employees, to foster alignment, minimize misunderstandings, and enhance collaboration.

Law 48, Page 137
Reflect, Learn, and Iterate
Foster a culture of reflection, continuous learning, and iteration to glean insights from past experiences, successes, and failures in GSA contracting and drive ongoing improvement and innovation.

The 48 Laws of GSA Contracting Conclusion

A note from the Author

Welcome to the comprehensive guidebook that navigates the intricacies, challenges, and strategies within the realm of General Services Administration (GSA) contracting. Spanning across 48 chapters, this book serves as a compendium of wisdom, insights, and best practices curated to empower organizations in their pursuit of success within the dynamic landscape of government contracting.

Within these pages, you will embark on a journey through the multifaceted world of GSA contracting, exploring topics ranging from strategic decision-making and negotiation tactics to stakeholder management and ethical conduct. Each chapter offers a nuanced perspective, drawing from years of experience, expertise, and real-world insights gathered from practitioners, experts, and thought leaders in the field.

As you delve into the chapters, you will encounter a rich tapestry of principles, strategies, and methodologies designed to equip organizations with the knowledge and tools necessary to thrive amidst the complexities of GSA contracting. From foundational principles to advanced techniques, each chapter is meticulously crafted to provide actionable guidance and practical solutions for navigating the challenges and seizing the opportunities inherent in government contracting.

Moreover, this book serves as a testament to the ever-evolving nature of GSA contracting, reflecting the dynamic interplay of regulations, market dynamics, and technological advancements shaping the landscape. It underscores the imperative of adaptability, innovation, and continuous learning as essential ingredients for success in the competitive GSA marketplace.

Whether you are a seasoned veteran seeking to refine your strategies or a newcomer embarking on your GSA contracting journey, this book offers a wealth of knowledge and insights to inform your endeavors. It is a testament to the collective wisdom and expertise of professionals committed to advancing the principles of integrity, excellence, and innovation within government contracting.

As you embark on this journey, may the chapters within serve as a source of inspiration, guidance, and empowerment, illuminating the path toward success and fulfillment in the dynamic world of General Services Administration contracting.

With warm regards,

The GovTikTalk Team

"The art of war is
to avoid battles."
SUN TZU

Law 1

Choose Your Battles Wisely: Understand which contracts are worth pursuing and which may not align with your long-term objectives.

In the realm of General Services Administration (GSA) contracting, the adage "Choose Your Battles Wisely" resonates profoundly. Every endeavor in this domain demands a strategic approach, where discernment and foresight pave the path to success.

Understanding the Terrain

Before embarking on any contract pursuit, it's imperative to comprehend the intricacies of the GSA landscape. Government contracts span a vast spectrum, ranging from defense to healthcare, each with its unique set of regulations, requirements, and opportunities.

Navigating this labyrinth requires meticulous planning and a keen eye for discerning prospects that align with your organization's long-term objectives. A contract that seems lucrative on the surface may not always be conducive to your overarching mission. Therefore, it's paramount to assess each opportunity through the lens of strategic alignment.

Aligning Objectives

The pursuit of GSA contracts should not be driven solely by short-term gains but rather by a coherent, long-term strategy. Each endeavor must complement your organization's mission, vision, and values, propelling it towards sustained growth and impact.

Before committing resources to a contract, conduct a thorough analysis to gauge its strategic fit. Consider factors such as the contract's duration, scope, potential for scalability, and alignment with your core competencies. Remember, not all contracts are created equal, and the decision to pursue or abstain requires careful deliberation.

Mitigating Risks

In the pursuit of GSA contracts, risks abound at every turn. From regulatory hurdles to market fluctuations, the landscape is fraught with uncertainties. Choosing your battles wisely entails not only identifying promising opportunities but also mitigating associated risks effectively.

Conduct comprehensive risk assessments, evaluating potential pitfalls and devising mitigation strategies proactively. Assess the political climate, economic trends, and regulatory landscape to anticipate potential challenges that may arise during contract execution.

Strategic Withdrawal

Equally important as identifying promising opportunities is recognizing when to disengage. Not all battles are meant to be fought, and strategic withdrawal can often be a prudent course of action. If a contract veers significantly from your organizational objectives or poses undue risks, it may be wiser to recalibrate your strategy and redirect resources elsewhere.

In the dynamic world of GSA contracting, adaptability is paramount. The ability to pivot swiftly in response to changing circumstances distinguishes the prudent strategist from the imprudent one.

Conclusion

In the pursuit of success within the GSA ecosystem, the imperative to "Choose Your Battles Wisely" serves as a guiding principle. By aligning pursuits with long-term objectives, mitigating risks judiciously, and exercising strategic discernment, organizations can navigate the labyrinth of government contracting with confidence and purpose.

"Knowledge is power."
FRANCIS BACON

Law 2

Know the Market and Your Competition: Research thoroughly to understand market trends, pricing strategies, and your competitors' strengths and weaknesses.

In the intricate dance of General Services Administration (GSA) contracting, knowledge is power. To thrive in this competitive arena, one must possess a deep understanding of market dynamics, emerging trends, and the ever-evolving landscape of competition.

The Essence of Market Intelligence

At the heart of effective GSA contracting lies the pursuit of market intelligence. Comprehensive research is the cornerstone upon which informed decisions are built. Organizations must invest time and resources into understanding market trends, customer preferences, and emerging technologies that shape the GSA landscape.

Through rigorous analysis and data-driven insights, organizations can identify untapped opportunities, anticipate shifting demand patterns, and position themselves strategically amidst the competitive fray.

Unraveling the Competition

In the cutthroat world of GSA contracting, competitors lurk at every turn, vying for the same coveted contracts and clients. To gain a competitive edge, one must meticulously dissect the strategies, strengths, and weaknesses of rival entities.

Conducting a thorough competitive analysis enables organizations to benchmark their performance, identify areas for improvement, and devise strategies to differentiate themselves in the marketplace. By discerning the unique value propositions of competitors, organizations can tailor their approaches to capitalize on unmet needs and carve out a distinct competitive advantage.

Harnessing the Power of Information

In the digital age, information reigns supreme. Organizations must leverage data analytics, market research, and competitive intelligence tools to glean actionable insights that drive strategic decision-making. By harnessing the power of information, organizations can identify emerging trends, anticipate customer needs, and pivot swiftly in response to market dynamics.

Moreover, by staying attuned to regulatory changes, policy shifts, and geopolitical developments, organizations can position themselves as agile and adaptive players within the GSA ecosystem. In a landscape characterized by uncertainty and volatility, knowledge truly becomes a formidable ally.

Strategic Positioning

Armed with a comprehensive understanding of the market and its competitors, organizations can craft robust strategies that position them for success. By identifying niche markets, cultivating strategic partnerships, and capitalizing on emerging trends, organizations can differentiate themselves and capture lucrative opportunities within the GSA marketplace.

Furthermore, by fostering a culture of innovation and continuous learning, organizations can stay ahead of the curve and adapt swiftly to changing market dynamics. In the ever-shifting terrain of GSA contracting, those who possess the foresight to anticipate trends and the agility to capitalize on opportunities will emerge victorious.

Conclusion

In the realm of GSA contracting, knowledge is the ultimate currency. By embracing the imperative to know the market and understand the competition, organizations can chart a course towards sustained success and prominence within the GSA ecosystem. Through strategic insights, informed decision-making, and relentless pursuit of excellence, organizations can navigate the complexities of the marketplace with confidence and clarity.

"Your network is your net worth."
PORTER GALE

Law 3

Build Strong Relationships: Cultivate relationships with key decision-makers within the GSA and client organizations to enhance your chances of success.

In the dynamic world of General Services Administration (GSA) contracting, success is not merely defined by transactions but by the strength of relationships forged along the way. Cultivating robust connections with key stakeholders within the GSA and client organizations forms the bedrock upon which enduring success is built.

The Power of Relationships

At its core, GSA contracting is a people-centric endeavor. Behind every contract, proposal, and negotiation lies a network of individuals whose trust, support, and influence can shape the trajectory of one's endeavors. Building strong relationships with key decision-makers within the GSA and client organizations is paramount to navigating the complex web of government contracting.

Understanding Stakeholder Dynamics

Effective relationship-building begins with a deep understanding of stakeholder dynamics. Identify the individuals and entities that wield influence within the GSA ecosystem, from procurement officers to agency heads, and cultivate meaningful connections with each. By understanding the motivations, priorities, and pain points of key stakeholders, organizations can tailor their approaches to resonate effectively and foster mutually beneficial partnerships.

Investing in Trust and Credibility

Trust is the currency of relationships, and credibility is its foundation. Organizations must demonstrate integrity, reliability, and transparency in all their interactions to earn the trust of stakeholders. Delivering on promises, upholding ethical standards, and maintaining open lines of communication are essential tenets of building trust within the GSA ecosystem.

Furthermore, organizations must invest in establishing themselves as credible partners capable of delivering exceptional value. Showcase past performance, accolades, and testimonials to instill confidence in prospective clients and position your organization as a trusted ally in their pursuit of mission success.

Nurturing Strategic Alliances

In the competitive landscape of GSA contracting, strategic alliances can be a potent force multiplier. Collaborate with complementary firms, industry associations, and advocacy groups to expand your reach, capabilities, and resources within the marketplace. By forging symbiotic partnerships, organizations can leverage synergies, share resources, and access new markets previously beyond their reach.

Sustaining Relationships Through Value Creation

Relationship-building is not a one-time endeavor but an ongoing commitment to value creation and mutual growth. Continuously engage with stakeholders, solicit feedback, and adapt your approaches to meet evolving needs and expectations. By demonstrating a genuine commitment to understanding and addressing the challenges faced by clients and partners, organizations can foster enduring relationships grounded in shared values and objectives.

Conclusion

In the realm of GSA contracting, relationships are the lifeblood of success. By investing in the cultivation of strong, meaningful connections with key stakeholders, organizations can unlock doors to new opportunities, navigate challenges with resilience, and achieve transformative impact within the GSA ecosystem. Through trust, credibility, and a relentless focus on value creation, organizations can forge relationships that stand the test of time and propel them towards sustained success in the dynamic world of government contracting.

"It is not the strongest of the species that survive, nor the most intelligent, but the one most responsive to change."
CHARLES DARWIN

Law 4

Adapt to Change: Be flexible and adaptive to changes in regulations, policies, and market dynamics affecting the GSA Multiple Award Schedule.

In the ever-evolving landscape of General Services Administration (GSA) contracting, the only constant is change. Regulatory frameworks shift, market dynamics fluctuate, and technological advancements reshape the terrain with unprecedented speed. To thrive in this dynamic environment, organizations must embrace adaptability as a guiding principle and navigate the winds of change with resilience and agility.

The Imperative of Adaptation

Adaptability is not merely a desirable trait but a strategic imperative in the realm of GSA contracting. Organizations must anticipate and embrace change as an inherent aspect of the contracting landscape, rather than viewing it as an obstacle to be overcome.

By cultivating a culture of adaptability and agility, organizations can position themselves to capitalize on emerging opportunities and mitigate the risks associated with uncertainty.

Navigating Regulatory Complexities

The regulatory landscape governing GSA contracting is subject to constant evolution, shaped by legislative mandates, executive directives, and judicial interpretations. Organizations must remain vigilant and proactive in monitoring regulatory changes, ensuring compliance, and adapting their strategies and processes accordingly. By staying abreast of regulatory developments, organizations can minimize compliance risks and capitalize on emerging opportunities within the GSA ecosystem.

Responding to Market Dynamics

Market dynamics within the GSA ecosystem are characterized by rapid shifts in demand, emerging trends, and evolving customer preferences. Organizations must maintain a finger on the pulse of market trends, leveraging data analytics and market intelligence to anticipate shifts in demand and capitalize on emerging opportunities. By remaining agile and responsive to market dynamics, organizations can position themselves as industry leaders and gain a competitive edge within the GSA marketplace.

Embracing Technological Innovation

Technological innovation is a driving force behind transformative change within the GSA ecosystem, revolutionizing processes, enhancing efficiency, and unlocking new avenues for growth. Organizations must embrace innovation as a catalyst for change, investing in emerging technologies and digital solutions that enable them to streamline operations, deliver value-added services, and differentiate themselves from competitors. By fostering a culture of innovation and embracing disruptive technologies, organizations can position themselves as pioneers within the GSA marketplace and drive sustainable growth in the digital age.

Cultivating Organizational Resilience

In the face of uncertainty and adversity, organizational resilience is paramount to survival and success. Organizations must cultivate resilience by fostering a culture of adaptability, empowering employees to embrace change, and fostering a spirit of innovation and continuous improvement. By equipping employees with the skills, tools, and mindset necessary to navigate change effectively, organizations can thrive amidst uncertainty and emerge stronger and more resilient in the face of adversity.

Conclusion

In the dynamic world of GSA contracting, adaptability is not a luxury but a necessity. By embracing change as a catalyst for growth, organizations can navigate the complexities of the contracting landscape with resilience and agility. Through vigilance, innovation, and a commitment to organizational excellence, organizations can position themselves as industry leaders and drive sustainable growth in the dynamic and ever-evolving world of government contracting.

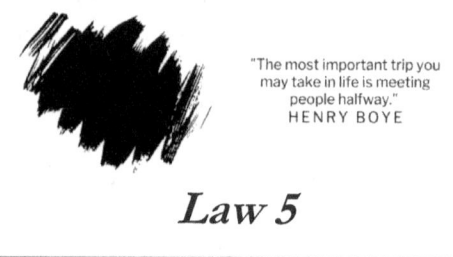

"The most important trip you may take in life is meeting people halfway."
HENRY BOYE

Law 5

Master the Art of Negotiation: Hone your negotiation skills to secure favorable terms, pricing, and conditions within GSA contracts.

In the intricate domain of General Services Administration (GSA) contracting, mastering the art of negotiation is paramount for organizations seeking to secure favorable terms, pricing, and conditions within GSA contracts. Negotiation skills play a pivotal role in navigating the complexities of contractual agreements, fostering collaboration, and achieving mutually beneficial outcomes for all parties involved.

Understanding the Dynamics of GSA Negotiations

Effective negotiation within the realm of GSA contracts requires a deep understanding of the dynamics at play, including regulatory constraints, budgetary considerations, and stakeholder interests. Organizations must conduct thorough research to comprehend the intricacies of GSA regulations, pricing methodologies, and competitive landscapes before entering negotiations.

Understanding the priorities and constraints of both GSA officials and client organizations is essential for crafting compelling proposals and negotiating favorable terms. By aligning their proposals with the needs and objectives of GSA stakeholders, organizations can enhance their negotiating leverage and increase the likelihood of successful outcomes.

Building Trust and Rapport

Building trust and rapport is fundamental to successful negotiations in GSA contracting. Trust forms the foundation of

productive relationships and fosters open communication, transparency, and collaboration throughout the negotiation process. Organizations must prioritize relationship-building efforts with GSA officials and client representatives to cultivate mutual respect and understanding.

Establishing trust involves demonstrating integrity, reliability, and a genuine commitment to meeting the needs of GSA stakeholders. By adhering to ethical standards, honoring commitments, and delivering on promises, organizations can earn the trust and confidence of GSA officials and enhance their negotiating position.

Effective Communication and Active Listening

Effective communication and active listening are indispensable skills for navigating negotiations within the GSA landscape.

Organizations must articulate their value proposition clearly, concisely, and persuasively, highlighting the unique benefits and advantages they offer in fulfilling GSA contracts. Clear communication helps clarify expectations, address concerns, and facilitate consensus among negotiating parties.

Equally important is the practice of active listening, which involves attentively understanding the perspectives, priorities, and concerns of GSA officials and client representatives. By listening actively, organizations can identify common ground, explore creative solutions, and build consensus around mutually beneficial outcomes in GSA negotiations.

Seeking Win-Win Solutions

In GSA negotiations, the pursuit of win-win solutions is essential for fostering long-term partnerships and driving sustainable value creation. Organizations must adopt a collaborative mindset, seeking outcomes that balance the interests and objectives of all parties involved. Win-win solutions prioritize fairness, equity, and mutual benefit, enabling GSA contracts to serve as catalysts for innovation, growth, and success.

Negotiating win-win solutions requires creativity, flexibility, and a willingness to explore alternative options and compromises. Organizations must approach negotiations with an open mind, valuing long-term relationships and shared objectives over short-term gains. By prioritizing win-win outcomes, organizations can forge strong alliances, mitigate conflicts, and unlock new opportunities for collaboration and growth within the GSA marketplace.

Conclusion

Mastering the art of negotiation is a cornerstone of success in General Services Administration (GSA) contracting. By understanding the dynamics of GSA negotiations, building trust and rapport, practicing effective communication and active listening, and seeking win-win solutions, organizations can navigate the complexities of GSA contracts with confidence, integrity, and resilience. In prioritizing effective negotiation strategies, organizations demonstrate their commitment to fostering productive relationships, driving value creation, and achieving enduring success in the competitive landscape of GSA contracting.

"Independence is happiness."
SUSAN B. ANTHONY

Law 6

Maintain Independence and Autonomy: Avoid overreliance on any single contract or client to maintain your independence and negotiating leverage.

In the intricate tapestry of General Services Administration (GSA) contracting, the allure of lucrative contracts can sometimes lead organizations down a perilous path of dependency. Overreliance on any single contract or client can erode autonomy, compromise negotiating leverage, and expose organizations to undue risks. To safeguard against such pitfalls, organizations must prioritize independence and autonomy as fundamental principles guiding their strategic decisions.

The Pitfalls of Overreliance

In the competitive landscape of GSA contracting, the temptation to secure long-term contracts with high-profile clients can be compelling. However, such contracts often come with strings attached, tethering organizations to the whims and demands of clients and compromising their autonomy in the process. Overreliance on any single contract or client can expose organizations to significant risks, including revenue volatility, contractual disputes, and loss of bargaining power.

Diversification as a Strategic Imperative

Diversification serves as a potent antidote to the perils of overreliance, enabling organizations to mitigate risks and fortify their resilience against market uncertainties. By diversifying their client base, service offerings, and revenue streams, organizations can reduce dependency on any single contract or client and insulate themselves from the adverse impacts of market fluctuations and contractual disputes.

Strategic diversification extends beyond client relationships to encompass geographic markets, industry sectors, and service delivery models. By embracing a diversified portfolio approach, organizations can capitalize on emerging opportunities, hedge against downside risks, and position themselves for sustained growth and success in the competitive landscape of GSA contracting.

Preserving Negotiating Leverage

Maintaining independence and autonomy affords organizations greater flexibility and negotiating leverage in their interactions with clients and partners. By cultivating a diverse portfolio of contracts and clients, organizations can negotiate from a position of strength, secure favorable terms and conditions, and drive value for their stakeholders.

Furthermore, independence empowers organizations to pursue strategic initiatives and investments that align with their long-term objectives, unconstrained by the dictates of any single contract or client. By preserving autonomy, organizations can unlock new growth opportunities, foster innovation, and differentiate themselves in the marketplace.

Balancing Risk and Reward

Independence and autonomy are not without their challenges, requiring organizations to strike a delicate balance between risk and reward. While diversification mitigates risks associated with over-reliance, it also necessitates careful resource allocation, strategic planning, and risk management.

Organizations must conduct rigorous risk assessments, monitor market dynamics, and adapt their strategies in response to changing circumstances. By embracing a prudent approach to risk management, organizations can navigate uncertainties with confidence, safeguard against potential threats, and capitalize on emerging opportunities within the GSA ecosystem.

Conclusion

In the competitive landscape of GSA contracting, independence and autonomy are indispensable assets that underpin organizational resilience, negotiating leverage, and long-term sustainability. By prioritizing independence, diversifying their portfolios, and embracing prudent risk management practices, organizations can navigate the complexities of the contracting landscape with confidence and emerge stronger and more resilient in the face of adversity.

"Innovation distinguishes between a leader and a follower."
STEVE JOBS

Law 7

Embrace Innovation: Continuously innovate your products, services, and solutions to stay relevant and competitive within the GSA marketplace.

In the dynamic world of General Services Administration (GSA) contracting, innovation is the catalyst for transformation and growth. Embracing innovation is not merely a choice but a strategic imperative for organizations seeking to thrive in the competitive landscape of government contracting. By continuously innovating their products, services, and solutions, organizations can stay relevant, competitive, and poised for success in the ever-evolving GSA marketplace.

The Imperative of Innovation

Innovation lies at the heart of progress, driving breakthroughs in technology, processes, and business models. In the context of GSA contracting, innovation is synonymous with adaptability, agility, and the ability to anticipate and respond to emerging trends and customer needs.

Embracing innovation enables organizations to differentiate themselves from competitors, unlock new sources of value, and drive operational efficiency. By challenging the status quo and embracing a culture of creativity and experimentation, organizations can position themselves as industry leaders and pioneers within the GSA ecosystem.

Fostering a Culture of Innovation

At its core, innovation is a mindset—an ethos that permeates every facet of organizational culture. Leaders must champion innovation as a core organizational value, encouraging employees to think outside the box, challenge conventional wisdom, and pursue bold ideas that push the boundaries of possibility.

Fostering a culture of innovation requires creating an environment that encourages risk-taking, rewards experimentation, and embraces failure as a natural byproduct of the innovation process. By empowering employees to unleash their creative potential, organizations can tap into a reservoir of untapped ideas and insights that drive transformative change and propel the organization forward.

Harnessing Technological Advancements

Technological advancements are a driving force behind innovation within the GSA ecosystem, offering new opportunities to streamline processes, enhance efficiency, and deliver value-added services to clients. Organizations must leverage emerging technologies such as artificial intelligence, data analytics, and blockchain to drive innovation across every aspect of their operations.

By harnessing the power of technology, organizations can automate routine tasks, unlock actionable insights from data, and deliver personalized experiences that exceed customer expectations. Furthermore, technology enables organizations to scale their operations, expand their reach, and unlock new revenue streams previously beyond their reach.

Collaborating for Innovation

Innovation thrives in environments where diverse perspectives converge, ideas collide, and collaboration flourishes. Organizations must embrace open innovation models that foster collaboration with clients, partners, and stakeholders across the GSA ecosystem. By co-creating solutions, sharing best practices, and tapping into collective intelligence, organizations can accelerate the pace of innovation and drive sustainable growth.

Strategic partnerships and alliances play a pivotal role in fostering innovation within the GSA marketplace, enabling organizations to leverage complementary strengths, access new markets, and co-innovate solutions that address complex challenges. By forging strategic alliances with industry leaders, startups, and academia, organizations can tap into a diverse ecosystem of expertise and resources that fuel innovation and drive competitive advantage.

Conclusion

Innovation is the lifeblood of progress, driving transformation, and growth within the GSA contracting landscape. By embracing innovation as a core organizational value, fostering a culture of creativity and experimentation, and harnessing the power of technology and collaboration, organizations can unlock new opportunities, drive operational excellence, and position themselves for sustained success in the dynamic and ever-evolving world of government contracting.

"Quality is not an act, it is a
habit."
ARISTOTLE

Law 8

Deliver Exceptional Value: Strive to exceed client expectations by consistently delivering high-quality products and services under GSA contracts.

In the realm of General Services Administration (GSA) contracting, the currency of success is measured not only in terms of contracts won but also in the value delivered to clients. To thrive in this competitive landscape, organizations must strive to exceed client expectations by consistently delivering exceptional value through their products and services under GSA contracts.

Understanding Client Needs

At the heart of delivering exceptional value lies a deep understanding of client needs, priorities, and pain points. Organizations must invest time and resources in building robust client relationships, soliciting feedback, and gaining insights into client preferences and expectations. By understanding the unique challenges faced by clients within the GSA ecosystem, organizations can tailor their offerings to address specific needs and deliver tangible value.

Quality as the Cornerstone

Quality serves as the cornerstone of value delivery, underpinning every aspect of the client experience. Organizations must adhere to rigorous quality standards, adhere to industry best practices, and strive for excellence in every interaction with clients. By maintaining a relentless focus on quality, organizations can instill confidence in clients, build trust, and differentiate themselves from competitors within the GSA marketplace.

Innovation as a Value Driver

Innovation is a potent driver of value creation within the GSA ecosystem, enabling organizations to deliver transformative solutions that address evolving client needs and preferences. Organizations must embrace a culture of innovation, encourage creativity, and empower employees to explore new ideas and approaches to problem-solving. By leveraging emerging technologies, processes, and business models, organizations can unlock new sources of value, drive operational efficiency, and enhance the client experience.

Customer-Centricity as a Guiding Principle

Delivering exceptional value requires a customer-centric approach that places the needs and preferences of clients at the forefront of decision-making. Organizations must adopt a proactive stance towards anticipating client needs, resolving issues promptly, and exceeding expectations at every touchpoint along the client journey. By prioritizing customer satisfaction and loyalty, organizations can foster long-term relationships, drive repeat business, and generate positive word-of-mouth referrals within the GSA marketplace.

Continuous Improvement as a Mindset

Excellence is not a destination but a journey—a relentless pursuit of continuous improvement and refinement. Organizations must embrace a mindset of continuous improvement, soliciting feedback, analyzing performance metrics, and identifying opportunities for enhancement. By fostering a culture of learning, adaptability, and innovation, organizations can stay ahead of the curve, anticipate client needs, and deliver value that exceeds expectations.

Conclusion

In the competitive landscape of GSA contracting, delivering exceptional value is not only a competitive advantage but a strategic imperative for success. By understanding client needs, prioritizing quality, fostering innovation, and embracing a customer-centric mindset, organizations can differentiate themselves from competitors, build lasting client relationships, and drive sustainable growth in the dynamic and ever-evolving world of government contracting.

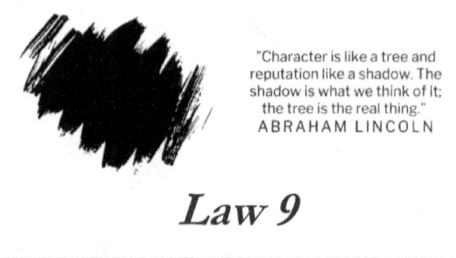

"Character is like a tree and reputation like a shadow. The shadow is what we think of it; the tree is the real thing."
ABRAHAM LINCOLN

Law 9

Protect Your Reputation: Guard your reputation and integrity fiercely, as they are crucial assets in the world of government contracting.

In the realm of General Services Administration (GSA) contracting, reputation is currency—an invaluable asset that can shape perceptions, influence decisions, and open doors to new opportunities. Guarding one's reputation fiercely is not only a matter of ethical responsibility but a strategic imperative for success in the competitive landscape of government contracting.

The Value of Reputation

A sterling reputation is a testament to an organization's integrity, reliability, and commitment to excellence. In the world of GSA contracting, reputation precedes and accompanies every interaction, serving a hallmark of trustworthiness and credibility. Organizations with strong reputations command respect, inspire confidence, and enjoy a competitive advantage in the marketplace.

Integrity as the Bedrock

Integrity is the foundation upon which reputations are built and preserved. Organizations must adhere unwaveringly to the highest ethical standards, conducting business with transparency, honesty, and fairness in all their dealings. By upholding integrity as a core organizational value, organizations can earn the trust and respect of clients, partners, and stakeholders within the GSA ecosystem.

Consistency in Performance

Consistency is key to maintaining a stellar reputation in the world of GSA contracting. Organizations must strive to deliver consistent, high-quality performance across every aspect of their operations—from contract execution to customer service. By setting clear expectations, meeting deadlines, and exceeding client expectations, organizations can reinforce their reputation for reliability and dependability.

Transparency and Accountability

Transparency breeds trust—a fundamental tenet of reputation management within the GSA marketplace. Organizations must operate with transparency, providing clear and accurate information to clients, partners, and stakeholders. In the event of challenges or setbacks, organizations must take ownership, demonstrate accountability, and proactively communicate with stakeholders to resolve issues and mitigate reputational risks.

Proactive Reputation Management

Reputation management is not a passive endeavor but a proactive effort to safeguard and enhance one's standing in the marketplace. Organizations must invest in proactive reputation management strategies, monitoring online conversations, soliciting feedback, and addressing concerns promptly and effectively. By actively managing their reputations, organizations can mitigate risks, capitalize on opportunities, and build a positive brand image that resonates with clients and stakeholders.

Commitment to Excellence

Excellence is the hallmark of a reputable organization—one that consistently strives for the highest standards of performance and professionalism. Organizations must foster a culture of excellence, encouraging employees to pursue excellence in every aspect of their work. By investing in employee training, professional development, and performance recognition, organizations can cultivate a workforce committed to upholding the organization's reputation for excellence.

Conclusion

In the competitive landscape of GSA contracting, reputation is a precious asset that must be safeguarded and nurtured with care. By upholding integrity, delivering consistent performance, operating with transparency and accountability, and fostering a culture of excellence, organizations can protect and enhance their reputations in the dynamic and ever-evolving world of government contracting. In doing so, they can position themselves for long-term success and prominence within the GSA marketplace.

"The art of communication is the language of leadership."
JAMES HUMES

Law 10

Communicate Effectively: Develop clear and concise communication strategies to convey your value proposition and differentiate yourself from competitors.

In the intricate web of General Services Administration (GSA) contracting, effective communication is the linchpin that facilitates understanding, fosters collaboration, and drives success. The ability to convey your value proposition clearly and persuasively can mean the difference between winning or losing contracts, building strong relationships, and standing out in the competitive landscape of government contracting.

Clarity and Conciseness

Effective communication begins with clarity and conciseness. In a complex and highly regulated environment like GSA contracting, clarity is paramount to ensuring that messages are understood accurately and completely. Organizations must distill complex concepts into clear, digestible nuggets of information that resonate with stakeholders across diverse backgrounds and levels of expertise.

Conciseness is equally essential, as brevity enhances comprehension and retention. By conveying information succinctly and eliminating unnecessary jargon, organizations can capture and maintain the attention of busy stakeholders inundated with information.

Tailoring Messages to Audiences

One size does not fit all when it comes to communication. Organizations must tailor their messages to resonate with different audiences, taking into account their unique needs, priorities, and communication preferences. Whether communicating with procurement officers, agency heads, or end-users, organizations must adopt a flexible approach that speaks directly to the interests and concerns of each stakeholder group.

By customizing messages to address specific pain points, highlight relevant benefits, and align with stakeholder priorities, organizations can forge deeper connections and foster meaningful engagement with their target audiences.

Utilizing Multiple Channels

Effective communication transcends traditional boundaries, encompassing a diverse array of channels and mediums. Organizations must leverage a mix of communication channels—from emails and phone calls to social media and in-person meetings—to reach stakeholders where they are and engage them effectively.

Moreover, organizations must adapt their communication strategies to align with the preferences and habits of different stakeholder groups. While some stakeholders may prefer formal written communications, others may respond better to informal conversations or interactive presentations. By diversifying communication channels and formats, organizations can maximize their reach and impact across diverse audiences.

Active Listening and Feedback

Communication is a two-way street, and effective communicators must not only convey their messages but also listen actively and solicit feedback from stakeholders. By listening attentively to stakeholder concerns, addressing questions and objections, and incorporating feedback into their communications, organizations can build trust, demonstrate empathy, and foster stronger relationships with their audiences.

Moreover, by actively seeking feedback, organizations can gain valuable insights into stakeholder perceptions, preferences, and priorities, enabling them to refine their communication strategies and tailor their messages more effectively in the future.

Conclusion

In the competitive landscape of GSA contracting, effective communication is a strategic imperative that underpins success. By prioritizing clarity and conciseness, tailoring messages to audiences, leveraging multiple communication channels, and actively listening to feedback, organizations can enhance their communication effectiveness, build stronger relationships, and differentiate themselves in the dynamic and ever-evolving world of government contracting. In doing so, they can position themselves for success and seize opportunities for growth and innovation within the GSA marketplace.

"True wisdom is knowing what you don't know and seeking to understand."
CONFUCIUS

Law 11

Leverage Information and Intelligence: Utilize market intelligence and data analytics to make informed decisions and gain a competitive edge.

In the intricate ecosystem of General Services Administration (GSA) contracting, information is power—a potent asset that can confer strategic advantages, inform decision-making, and drive success. By harnessing market intelligence, data analytics, and actionable insights, organizations can gain a competitive edge, anticipate trends, and navigate the complexities of the GSA marketplace with confidence and precision.

The Power of Market Intelligence

Market intelligence serves as a compass in the turbulent seas of government contracting, guiding organizations toward lucrative opportunities and away from potential pitfalls. By monitoring market trends, analyzing competitor strategies, and assessing client preferences, organizations can gain a nuanced understanding of the dynamics shaping the GSA landscape and position themselves strategically to capitalize on emerging opportunities.

Market intelligence enables organizations to identify unmet needs, forecast demand patterns, and tailor their offerings to align with client expectations effectively. By leveraging insights gleaned from market intelligence, organizations can optimize resource allocation, refine their value proposition, and stay ahead of the curve in the fiercely competitive world of government contracting.

Data Analytics as a Strategic Tool

In the era of big data, organizations are awash in a sea of information—a vast reservoir of untapped potential waiting to be unlocked. Data analytics empowers organizations to extract actionable insights from disparate datasets, uncover hidden patterns, and make informed decisions based on evidence and analysis.

By harnessing the power of data analytics, organizations can optimize pricing strategies, identify cost-saving opportunities, and enhance operational efficiency across every facet of their operations. From predictive modeling to trend analysis, data analytics equips organizations with the tools they need to navigate uncertainty, mitigate risks, and drive sustainable growth in the dynamic world of GSA contracting.

Strategic Decision-Making

In the fast-paced world of government contracting, strategic decision-making is paramount to success. Organizations must leverage information and intelligence to inform their decision-making processes, identify strategic priorities, and allocate resources effectively.

By integrating market intelligence and data analytics into their decision-making frameworks, organizations can make data-driven decisions that are grounded in evidence and aligned with their long-term objectives. Whether evaluating new market opportunities, assessing risk profiles, or optimizing resource allocation, organizations can leverage information and intelligence to make informed decisions that drive value and propel them toward their goals.

Continuous Learning and Adaptation

The GSA landscape is constantly evolving, shaped by regulatory changes, market dynamics, and geopolitical forces. Organizations must embrace a mindset of continuous learning and adaptation, leveraging information and intelligence to stay abreast of emerging trends and evolving client needs.

By investing in ongoing education, training, and professional development, organizations can equip their teams with the skills and expertise needed to thrive in an environment of constant change. By fostering a culture of curiosity and innovation, organizations can position themselves as agile and adaptive players within the

GSA ecosystem, ready to seize opportunities and overcome challenges in pursuit of their mission.

Conclusion

In the competitive landscape of GSA contracting, information and intelligence are indispensable assets that underpin success. By harnessing market intelligence, leveraging data analytics, and making informed decisions, organizations can gain a competitive edge, drive strategic growth, and achieve enduring success in the dynamic and ever-evolving world of government contracting. In doing so, they can unlock new opportunities, mitigate risks, and position themselves as leaders within the GSA marketplace.

"Patience, persistence, and perspiration make an unbeatable combination for success."
NAPOLEON HILL

Law 12

Cultivate Patience and Persistence: Understand that success in GSA contracting often requires long-term dedication, patience, and persistence.

In the labyrinthine world of General Services Administration (GSA) contracting, patience and persistence are not merely virtues but strategic imperatives. Success in GSA contracting often demands unwavering dedication, resilience in the face of setbacks, and a steadfast commitment to long-term goals. By cultivating patience and persistence, organizations can weather the challenges, navigate the complexities, and ultimately achieve success in the competitive landscape of government contracting.

The Long and Winding Road

GSA contracting is a journey fraught with challenges, uncertainties, and obstacles. From the arduous process of proposal submission to the labyrinthine corridors of bureaucratic red tape, organizations must navigate a myriad of hurdles on the path to securing GSA contracts. Patience is the key to endurance the steadfast resolve to persevere in the face of adversity and setbacks along the way.

Navigating the Procurement Process

The procurement process within the GSA ecosystem is characterized by its complexity and unpredictability. Organizations must navigate a maze of regulations, requirements, and procedural intricacies, often facing delays, rejections, and unexpected roadblocks along the way. Persistence is the fuel that drives progress—the unwavering determination to overcome obstacles, learn from failures, and press forward in pursuit of success.

Building Relationships and Trust

In the world of government contracting, relationships are currency—a testament to trust, reliability, and credibility. Building strong relationships with key stakeholders within the GSA and client organizations requires time, effort, and patience. Organizations must invest in nurturing connections, fostering trust, and demonstrating their commitment to delivering value over the long term.

By cultivating enduring relationships built on a foundation of integrity and mutual respect, organizations can position themselves as trusted partners and allies within the GSA ecosystem. Persistence is the bridge that spans the gap between initial contact and lasting partnership—the dogged pursuit of opportunities, the willingness to weather rejection, and the resilience to keep knocking on doors until they open.

Embracing the Journey

Success in GSA contracting is not defined by quick wins or instant gratification but by the journey itself—the trials, tribulations, and triumphs along the way. Organizations must embrace the journey with a spirit of patience and persistence, recognizing that progress often unfolds gradually, and success is the culmination of sustained effort and dedication.

By embracing patience and persistence as guiding principles, organizations can navigate the twists and turns of the GSA contracting landscape with resilience and resolve. In doing so, they can overcome adversity, seize opportunities, and achieve enduring success in the dynamic and ever-evolving world of government contracting.

Conclusion

In the competitive landscape of GSA contracting, patience and persistence are the cornerstones of success. By cultivating patience in the face of adversity and persistence in pursuit of long-term goals, organizations can weather the challenges, navigate the complexities, and ultimately emerge victorious in the pursuit of government contracts. In embracing the journey with resilience and resolve, organizations can achieve enduring success and establish themselves as leaders within the GSA marketplace.

"Risk comes from not knowing what you're doing."
WARREN BUFFETT

Law 13

Manage Risk Prudently: Identify, assess, and mitigate risks associated with GSA contracts to protect your business interests and ensure compliance.

In the high-stakes arena of General Services Administration (GSA) contracting, risk lurks at every turn, ready to derail even the most meticulously crafted plans. Prudent risk management is not merely a defensive strategy but a strategic imperative for organizations seeking to thrive in the competitive landscape of government contracting. By identifying, assessing, and mitigating risks proactively, organizations can protect their interests, preserve their reputation, and navigate the complexities of GSA contracting with confidence and resilience.

Understanding Risk in GSA Contracting

Risk pervades every aspect of GSA contracting, from proposal submission to contract execution and beyond. Organizations must adopt a holistic approach to risk management, recognizing that risks can manifest in myriad forms—financial, operational, legal, reputational, and strategic.

Uncertainties abound in the GSA landscape, ranging from changes in regulatory frameworks and budgetary constraints to shifts in market dynamics and geopolitical factors. Organizations must anticipate and prepare for these uncertainties, identifying potential risks and developing strategies to mitigate their impact.

Identifying Risks

The first step in effective risk management is the identification of potential risks that may threaten the success of GSA contracts. Organizations must conduct comprehensive risk assessments, analyzing internal and external factors that may pose threats or create vulnerabilities.

Common risks in GSA contracting include compliance failures, contract disputes, budgetary constraints, scope creep, cybersecurity threats, and supplier dependencies. By conducting thorough risk assessments, organizations can gain insights into potential vulnerabilities and develop strategies to mitigate or transfer risks effectively.

Assessing Risk Exposure

Once risks have been identified, organizations must assess their potential impact and likelihood of occurrence. Risk assessment involves evaluating the severity of potential consequences, the probability of occurrence, and the organization's tolerance for risk.

By quantifying and prioritizing risks based on their potential impact and likelihood, organizations can focus their resources and attention on mitigating high-priority risks that pose the greatest threat to contract success. Risk assessment provides organizations with valuable insights into the nature of risks they face and informs decision-making processes related to risk mitigation and contingency planning.

Mitigating Risks

Risk mitigation involves the implementation of strategies and controls to reduce the likelihood of risk occurrence or minimize its impact if it does occur. Organizations must develop robust risk mitigation plans tailored to address specific risks identified during the risk assessment process.

Mitigation strategies may include implementing internal controls, diversifying supplier relationships, securing insurance coverage, establishing contingency plans, and conducting regular audits and assessments. By proactively addressing potential risks, organizations can reduce vulnerabilities, enhance resilience, and safeguard their interests in the dynamic and uncertain environment of GSA contracting.

Monitoring and Adaptation

Risk management is an ongoing process that requires continuous monitoring, evaluation, and adaptation. Organizations must remain vigilant, monitoring changes in the GSA landscape, regulatory requirements, market dynamics, and emerging threats that may impact contract performance.

By establishing mechanisms for ongoing risk monitoring and reporting, organizations can detect early warning signs of potential risks and take corrective action before they escalate into crises. Moreover, organizations must remain agile and adaptive, adjusting their risk management strategies in response to changing circumstances and evolving threats.

Conclusion

In the competitive and dynamic world of GSA contracting, prudent risk management is a critical determinant of success. By identifying, assessing, and mitigating risks proactively, organizations can protect their interests, preserve their reputation, and navigate the complexities of government contracting with confidence and resilience. In embracing risk management as a strategic imperative, organizations can position themselves for success and achieve enduring excellence in the pursuit of GSA contracts.

"Alone we can do so little;
together we can do so much."
HELEN KELLER

Law 14

Foster Strategic Alliances: Form strategic partnerships and alliances with complementary firms to enhance your capabilities and broaden your reach within the GSA ecosystem.

In the intricate ecosystem of General Services Administration (GSA) contracting, strategic alliances serve as catalysts for growth, innovation, and success. By forging partnerships and alliances with complementary firms, organizations can expand their capabilities, leverage shared resources, and unlock new opportunities within the competitive landscape of government contracting.

The Power of Collaboration

Strategic alliances are founded on the principle of collaboration—a shared commitment to mutual success and shared goals. In the world of GSA contracting, where complexity and scale often exceed the capabilities of individual organizations, strategic alliances offer a pathway to greater efficiency, agility, and competitiveness.

By pooling their expertise, resources, and networks, organizations can achieve synergies that are greater than the sum of their parts. Strategic alliances enable organizations to access new markets, expand their service offerings, and differentiate themselves in the marketplace, positioning them for sustained growth and success.

Forming Strategic Partnerships

Strategic partnerships are built on a foundation of trust, shared values, and mutual respect. Organizations must identify potential partners whose capabilities, expertise, and market presence complement their own. Whether collaborating with industry peers, technology providers, or research institutions, organizations must seek out partners who bring unique strengths and perspectives to the table.

Effective partnerships are characterized by open communication, clear expectations, and a shared vision for success. Organizations must invest time and effort in nurturing relationships, aligning interests, and fostering collaboration at every level of the partnership.

Unlocking Synergies

Strategic alliances unlock synergies that drive innovation, efficiency, and growth. By combining complementary strengths and capabilities, organizations can achieve economies of scale, reduce costs, and enhance operational efficiency. Strategic alliances enable organizations to access new markets, penetrate new industries, and diversify their revenue streams, mitigating risks and creating new avenues for growth.

Moreover, strategic alliances facilitate knowledge sharing, cross-pollination of ideas, and collaborative problem-solving. By tapping into the collective intelligence of their partners, organizations can innovate more rapidly, respond to market changes more effectively, and deliver greater value to their clients.

Navigating Complex Ecosystems

The GSA contracting ecosystem is characterized by its complexity, diversity, and interdependence. Strategic alliances provide organizations with a roadmap for navigating this intricate landscape, enabling them to leverage the strengths and expertise of their partners to overcome challenges and capitalize on opportunities.

Strategic alliances also offer organizations a platform for advocacy and collective action. By joining forces with like-minded partners, organizations can amplify their voice, shape industry standards, and advocate for policies that support their collective interests.

Conclusion

In the competitive and dynamic world of GSA contracting, strategic alliances are indispensable assets that drive growth, innovation, and success. By fostering strategic partnerships, organizations can expand their capabilities, unlock synergies, and navigate the complexities of government contracting with confidence and resilience. In embracing collaboration as a strategic imperative, organizations can position themselves for sustained success and achieve enduring excellence in the competitive landscape of GSA contracting.

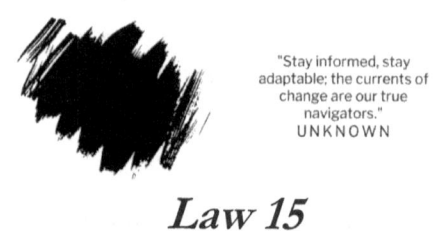

"Stay informed, stay adaptable; the currents of change are our true navigators."
UNKNOWN

Law 15

Stay Informed and Adaptable: Keep abreast of changes in GSA regulations, policies, and procedures to adapt your strategies accordingly.

In the ever-evolving landscape of General Services Administration (GSA) contracting, staying informed and adaptable is not just a strategy but a necessity for survival and success. The GSA environment is subject to constant change, characterized by shifting regulations, emerging technologies, and evolving client needs. By remaining vigilant, proactive, and adaptable, organizations can navigate the complexities of government contracting with agility and resilience.

The Imperative of Awareness

Awareness is the first line of defense in the volatile world of GSA contracting. Organizations must stay abreast of changes in regulations, policies, and market trends that may impact their operations and strategies. Vigilance is key, as even minor shifts in the regulatory landscape or competitive environment can have far-reaching implications for organizations competing for GSA contracts.

Organizations must cultivate a culture of continuous learning and information sharing, encouraging employees to stay informed about industry developments, best practices, and emerging technologies. By fostering a culture of awareness, organizations can empower their teams to anticipate change, adapt proactively, and seize opportunities for growth and innovation.

Adaptability as a Competitive Advantage

In the fast-paced world of GSA contracting, adaptability is a critical determinant of success. Organizations must be nimble and responsive, capable of adjusting their strategies and operations in real-time to address evolving client needs and market dynamics. Adaptability enables organizations to thrive in environments of uncertainty, volatility, and disruption, turning challenges into opportunities for growth and innovation.

To foster adaptability, organizations must embrace a mindset of flexibility, experimentation, and continuous improvement. Leaders must encourage creative thinking, empower employees to take calculated risks, and reward innovation and agility. By fostering a culture of adaptability, organizations can position themselves as agile and resilient players within the GSA ecosystem, ready to navigate uncertainty and seize opportunities for growth and success.

Strategic Information Management

In the era of big data and analytics, information is a powerful tool for decision-making and strategic planning. Organizations must leverage technology and data analytics to gather, analyze, and interpret information about market trends, client preferences, and competitor strategies. By harnessing the power of data-driven insights, organizations can make informed decisions, identify emerging opportunities, and optimize their strategies for success.

Strategic information management also involves risk assessment and scenario planning. Organizations must anticipate potential risks and develop contingency plans to mitigate their impact. By proactively identifying risks and developing response strategies, organizations can minimize disruption, protect their interests, and maintain continuity of operations in the face of adversity.

Conclusion

In the competitive and dynamic world of GSA contracting, staying informed and adaptable is essential for success. By cultivating awareness, fostering adaptability, and leveraging strategic information management practices, organizations can navigate the complexities of government contracting with confidence and resilience. In embracing a proactive approach to change and innovation, organizations can position themselves for sustained success and achieve enduring excellence in the competitive landscape of GSA contracting.

"In the marathon of life, think not of the mile but the journey's end."
UNKNOWN

Law 16

Think Long-Term: Adopt a long-term perspective in your approach to GSA contracting, focusing on building sustainable relationships and achieving enduring success.

In the intricate landscape of General Services Administration (GSA) contracting, thinking long-term is not just a strategy but a mindset that guides decision-making, shapes relationships, and drives success. The allure of short-term gains must be tempered by a steadfast commitment to building sustainable relationships, fostering innovation, and achieving enduring success in the competitive arena of government contracting.

The Essence of Long-Term Thinking

Long-term thinking transcends the immediate horizon, encompassing strategic planning, relationship building, and value creation over an extended timeframe. Organizations must resist the temptation to prioritize short-term gains at the expense of long-term sustainability and resilience. Instead, they must adopt a holistic perspective that considers the broader implications of their actions and decisions on their future success and viability.

Long-term thinking requires patience, foresight, and discipline. It involves setting ambitious but achievable goals, developing robust strategies, and investing in capabilities and relationships that will pay dividends over time. By embracing a long-term mindset, organizations can position themselves for sustained growth, resilience, and relevance in the dynamic and ever-evolving world of government contracting.

Building Sustainable Relationships

At the heart of long-term thinking lies the cultivation of sustainable relationships built on trust, integrity, and mutual respect. Organizations must prioritize relationship building as a strategic imperative, investing time and resources in nurturing connections with clients, partners, and stakeholders across the GSA ecosystem.

Building sustainable relationships requires a commitment to transparency, open communication, and collaboration. Organizations must demonstrate their value proposition, deliver on promises, and anticipate and address the evolving needs and preferences of their partners and clients. By fostering long-term relationships based on shared values and goals, organizations can create a network of allies and advocates who champion their interests and contribute to their long-term success.

Fostering Innovation and Adaptability

Long-term thinking necessitates a culture of innovation and adaptability that embraces change, fosters creativity, and drives continuous improvement. Organizations must invest in research and development, encourage experimentation, and empower employees to challenge the status quo and explore new ideas and approaches.

Innovation is the engine of long-term success, enabling organizations to anticipate market trends, capitalize on emerging opportunities, and stay ahead of the competition. By fostering a culture of innovation, organizations can adapt to evolving client needs, differentiate themselves in the marketplace, and create value that endures over time.

Strategic Planning and Resilience

Long-term thinking requires disciplined strategic planning that aligns short-term actions with long-term objectives and aspirations. Organizations must develop clear, actionable strategies that anticipate future challenges, leverage emerging opportunities, and capitalize on their core strengths and capabilities.

Strategic planning also involves building resilience and agility to navigate uncertainty and volatility in the GSA contracting landscape. Organizations must anticipate potential risks, develop contingency plans, and maintain flexibility to adapt to changing market dynamics and client requirements. By building resilience into their operations and strategies, organizations can withstand adversity, seize opportunities, and thrive in the face of uncertainty.

Conclusion

In the competitive and dynamic world of GSA contracting, thinking long-term is a strategic imperative that drives success and sustainability. By prioritizing sustainable relationships, fostering innovation and adaptability, and embracing disciplined strategic planning, organizations can position themselves for enduring success in the ever-evolving landscape of government contracting. In cultivating a long-term mindset, organizations can chart a course toward resilience, relevance, and excellence in the competitive arena of GSA contracting.

"The only thing necessary for the triumph of evil is for good men to do nothing."
EDMUND BURKE

Law 17

Remain Vigilant Against Corruption: Maintain high ethical standards and vigilance against corruption or unethical practices that may jeopardize your business reputation or GSA contracts.

In the realm of General Services Administration (GSA) contracting, integrity is the bedrock upon which trust is built, and corruption poses a grave threat to the integrity of the procurement process and the public trust. Vigilance against corruption is not only a moral imperative but a legal and ethical obligation for organizations seeking to uphold the principles of transparency, fairness, and accountability in government contracting.

The Impact of Corruption

Corruption undermines the integrity of the GSA contracting process, erodes public trust, and distorts market dynamics. From bribery and kickbacks to bid rigging and collusion, corrupt practices distort competition, inflate costs, and deprive taxpayers of the benefits of fair and open competition.

Corruption also tarnishes the reputation of organizations involved in government contracting, leading to financial losses, legal liabilities, and damage to brand equity. Moreover, corruption undermines the credibility of the procurement process, eroding confidence in government institutions and jeopardizing the public interest.

Ethical Standards and Compliance

Vigilance against corruption begins with a commitment to ethical standards and compliance with laws, regulations, and industry best practices. Organizations must establish robust compliance programs that promote a culture of integrity, transparency, and accountability throughout the organization.

Compliance programs should include clear policies and procedures for detecting, reporting, and addressing potential instances of corruption or unethical behavior. Employees must receive regular training on ethical standards, anti-corruption laws, and their obligations under the organization's compliance program.

Transparency and Accountability

Transparency is a powerful antidote to corruption, enabling stakeholders to scrutinize procurement processes, detect irregularities, and hold accountable those responsible for corrupt practices. Organizations must embrace transparency in their dealings with government agencies, clients, suppliers, and partners, disclosing relevant information and maintaining accurate records of transactions.

Accountability is essential for deterring corruption and ensuring that individuals and organizations are held responsible for their actions. Organizations must establish clear lines of authority and accountability, enforce consequences for unethical behavior, and provide mechanisms for reporting suspected instances of corruption anonymously and without fear of retaliation.

Due Diligence and Risk Management

Vigilance against corruption requires due diligence and risk management processes that identify, assess, and mitigate corruption risks throughout the procurement lifecycle. Organizations must conduct thorough background checks on potential business partners, suppliers, and contractors to identify any red flags or potential conflicts of interest.

Risk management strategies should include controls and safeguards to prevent corruption, such as competitive bidding processes, conflict-of-interest policies, and independent oversight mechanisms. Organizations must also monitor and audit procurement activities regularly to detect and address any signs of corruption or unethical behavior.

Conclusion

In the competitive and high-stakes arena of GSA contracting, vigilance against corruption is paramount to preserving the integrity of the procurement process and upholding public trust. By promoting ethical standards, transparency, and accountability, organizations can safeguard against corruption, mitigate risks, and demonstrate their commitment to the principles of fairness, integrity, and accountability in government contracting. In remaining vigilant against corruption, organizations can uphold the public trust, protect their reputation, and contribute to a fair and competitive marketplace for GSA contracts.

"Understand power, wield it wisely; for it can build bridges or burn them down."
UNKNOWN

Law 18

Be Mindful of Power Dynamics: Understand the power dynamics at play within the GSA environment and leverage them to your advantage ethically.

Within the complex ecosystem of General Services Administration (GSA) contracting, power dynamics play a significant role in shaping relationships, influencing decisions, and driving outcomes. Organizations must be mindful of the underlying power dynamics at play within the GSA environment and navigate them ethically and strategically to maximize their effectiveness and achieve their objectives.

Understanding Power Dynamics

Power in the context of GSA contracting can take many forms—financial resources, organizational influence, political connections, and expertise, among others. Different stakeholders wield varying degrees of power, and understanding these dynamics is essential for organizations seeking to navigate the procurement process successfully.

Government agencies, procurement officials, and contracting officers hold significant power in the GSA ecosystem, shaping procurement policies, making contract award decisions, and overseeing contract performance. Prime contractors and large corporations may also wield considerable influence due to their financial resources, market dominance, and established relationships with government agencies.

Ethical Considerations

While power can confer advantages in the competitive landscape of government contracting, organizations must exercise power ethically and responsibly. Ethical considerations should guide interactions with stakeholders, including government agencies, clients, partners, and competitors.

Organizations must avoid abusing their power or engaging in coercive tactics that undermine fairness, transparency, and competition in the procurement process. Instead, they should seek to build collaborative relationships based on trust, mutual respect, and shared goals. Ethical behavior not only preserves the integrity of the procurement process but also enhances organizational reputation and credibility within the GSA ecosystem.

Leveraging Power Ethically

Ethical use of power involves leveraging influence and resources to achieve positive outcomes for all stakeholders involved. Organizations should use their power responsibly to promote fairness, foster innovation, and drive value creation within the GSA contracting process.

For example, organizations can leverage their expertise and resources to develop innovative solutions that address client needs effectively. They can also use their influence to advocate for policies and practices that promote transparency, accountability, and integrity in government contracting.

Mitigating Power Imbalances

In cases where power imbalances exist, organizations must take proactive steps to mitigate their impact and level the playing field for all stakeholders. This may involve implementing policies and practices that promote diversity, equity, and inclusion in the procurement process, ensuring that small businesses and disadvantaged enterprises have equal opportunities to compete for GSA contracts.

Organizations should also seek to empower stakeholders with less power by providing them with access to resources, information, and support to enhance their capabilities and competitiveness in the marketplace.

Conclusion

In the competitive and complex world of GSA contracting, being mindful of power dynamics is essential for organizations seeking to navigate the procurement process successfully. By understanding power dynamics, exercising power ethically, and mitigating power imbalances, organizations can foster fairness, transparency, and integrity in government contracting. In doing so, they can build trust, enhance collaboration, and contribute to a competitive and equitable marketplace for GSA contracts.

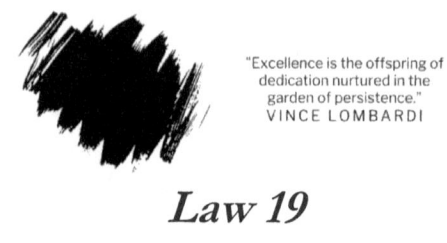

"Excellence is the offspring of
dedication nurtured in the
garden of persistence."
VINCE LOMBARDI

Law 19

Foster a Culture of Excellence: Cultivate a culture of excellence and continuous improvement within your organization to excel in GSA contracting.

In the competitive arena of General Services Administration (GSA) contracting, excellence is not merely an aspiration but a guiding principle that defines organizational culture, shapes behavior, and drives performance. Fostering a culture of excellence is essential for organizations seeking to differentiate themselves, deliver exceptional value, and achieve enduring success in the dynamic and ever-evolving world of government contracting.

Defining Excellence

Excellence encompasses a relentless pursuit of quality, innovation, and continuous improvement in every aspect of operations and client interactions. It is reflected in the organization's commitment to exceeding expectations, embracing best practices, and delivering superior outcomes that drive value and foster client satisfaction.

At its core, excellence is about setting high standards, holding oneself accountable to those standards, and continuously raising the bar for performance and achievement. It requires a mindset of continuous learning, adaptability, and a relentless focus on delivering exceptional results.

Cultivating a Culture of Excellence

Cultivating a culture of excellence begins with leadership—a commitment from top management to uphold the highest standards of integrity, professionalism, and accountability. Leaders must articulate a clear vision of excellence, inspire employees to embrace excellence as a core value, and lead by example through their words and actions.

Organizations must create an environment that fosters creativity, innovation, and collaboration, empowering employees to take ownership of their work, pursue excellence in everything they do, and contribute to the organization's success. This involves providing opportunities for professional development, recognizing and rewarding excellence, and fostering a culture of trust, respect, and transparency.

Continuous Improvement and Innovation

Excellence is a journey, not a destination, and organizations must embrace a mindset of continuous improvement and innovation to stay ahead of the curve in the competitive landscape of government contracting. This involves encouraging employees to challenge the status quo, experiment with new ideas and approaches, and learn from both successes and failures.

Organizations should create channels for feedback and idea sharing, fostering a culture of open communication and constructive dialogue that empowers employees to contribute their insights and expertise. By encouraging a spirit of innovation and experimentation, organizations can drive creativity, inspire breakthroughs, and position themselves as leaders in the field of GSA contracting.

Client-Centric Focus

Excellence in GSA contracting requires a relentless focus on client satisfaction and value creation. Organizations must understand their clients' needs, anticipate their expectations, and go above and beyond to exceed them. This involves delivering superior products, services, and solutions that address client pain points, solve complex problems, and drive tangible outcomes.

By prioritizing client satisfaction and building long-term relationships based on trust and mutual respect, organizations can differentiate themselves in the marketplace and position themselves for sustained success in the competitive landscape of government contracting.

Conclusion

In the competitive and challenging world of GSA contracting, fostering a culture of excellence is essential for organizations seeking to thrive and succeed. By setting high standards, embracing continuous improvement and innovation, and prioritizing client satisfaction, organizations can differentiate themselves, drive value, and achieve enduring success in the dynamic and ever-evolving world of government contracting. In cultivating a culture of excellence, organizations can inspire greatness, empower their employees, and position themselves as leaders in the field of GSA contracting.

"The measure of intelligence is the ability to change."
ALBERT EINSTEIN

Law 20

Adaptability over Rigidity: Be adaptable and willing to adjust your strategies and approaches based on evolving GSA requirements and market conditions.

In the dynamic and ever-evolving landscape of General Services Administration (GSA) contracting, adaptability reigns supreme as organizations navigate through shifting regulations, emerging technologies, and evolving client needs. In contrast, rigidity can prove to be detrimental, hindering organizations from seizing opportunities, responding to challenges, and thriving in the competitive environment of government contracting.

Embracing Change

Adaptability is the ability to respond effectively to change, uncertainty, and adversity. Organizations must recognize that change is inevitable in the GSA contracting landscape, driven by factors such as regulatory updates, technological advancements, and shifts in client preferences. Rather than resisting change, organizations should embrace it as an opportunity for growth, innovation, and evolution.

By fostering a culture of adaptability, organizations can empower employees to embrace change, experiment with new ideas, and explore innovative solutions to emerging challenges. This mindset encourages flexibility, creativity, and resilience, enabling organizations to navigate uncertainty with confidence and agility.

Flexibility in Strategies and Approaches

Adaptability requires organizations to be flexible in their strategies and approaches to GSA contracting. This involves being open to new ideas, alternative methods, and unconventional solutions that may better align with evolving client needs and market dynamics. Organizations must be willing to pivot quickly, adjust their course of action, and seize opportunities as they arise.

Rather than adhering rigidly to predetermined plans and processes, organizations should adopt a mindset of flexibility and experimentation. This may involve exploring new market segments, diversifying service offerings, or leveraging emerging technologies to gain a competitive edge in the GSA marketplace.

Learning from Feedback and Experience

Adaptability also entails a willingness to learn from feedback and past experiences. Organizations must be receptive to constructive criticism, client input, and market feedback, using this information to refine their strategies, improve their offerings, and enhance their performance in GSA contracting.

By fostering a culture of continuous learning and improvement, organizations can leverage insights gained from past successes and failures to inform future decision-making and strategy development. This iterative approach enables organizations to evolve over time, adapting to changing circumstances and emerging trends in the GSA landscape.

Agility in Execution

Adaptability is not just about being open to change—it's also about executing swiftly and decisively in response to changing circumstances. Organizations must be agile in their decision-making and execution, capable of mobilizing resources, reallocating priorities, and adjusting their approach in real-time to address emerging challenges and opportunities.

By empowering employees with the autonomy and authority to make decisions at the frontline, organizations can foster a culture of agility and responsiveness that enables them to stay ahead of the curve in the fast-paced world of GSA contracting.

Conclusion

In the competitive and dynamic environment of GSA contracting, adaptability is a critical determinant of success. By embracing change, fostering flexibility, learning from feedback and experience, and promoting agility in execution, organizations can position themselves for sustained success and achieve enduring excellence in the ever-evolving landscape of government contracting. In prioritizing adaptability over rigidity, organizations can navigate uncertainty with confidence, seize opportunities for growth, and thrive in the competitive arena of GSA contracting.

"Knowledge speaks, but
wisdom listens."
JIMI HENDRIX

Law 21

Demonstrate Expertise and Authority: Establish yourself as a trusted authority and thought leader within your niche or industry segment to enhance your credibility and influence within the GSA marketplace.

In the intricate realm of General Services Administration (GSA) contracting, establishing oneself as a trusted authority and thought leader is paramount to gaining credibility, influencing decision-makers, and securing lucrative contracts. Demonstrating expertise and authority not only enhances organizational reputation but also positions organizations as valuable partners within the GSA ecosystem.

Building Domain Expertise

Domain expertise forms the foundation of credibility and authority within the GSA contracting landscape. Organizations must invest in developing deep knowledge and understanding of government procurement processes, regulations, and industry best practices. This expertise enables organizations to provide valuable insights, strategic guidance, and innovative solutions to clients and stakeholders.

Building domain expertise requires a commitment to ongoing learning, professional development, and engagement with industry forums, conferences, and thought leadership platforms. Organizations must stay abreast of emerging trends, regulatory changes, and market developments, positioning themselves as trusted advisors and subject matter experts within the GSA ecosystem.

Thought Leadership and Influence

Thought leadership is about more than just sharing knowledge—it's about shaping conversations, driving innovation, and influencing the direction of the industry. Organizations must establish themselves as thought leaders by contributing thought-provoking insights, original research, and innovative ideas that challenge conventional wisdom and inspire change.

Thought leadership can take many forms, including white papers, research reports, blog posts, webinars, and speaking engagements at industry events. By sharing their expertise and perspectives with a wider audience, organizations can elevate their profile, expand their influence, and position themselves as leaders in the field of GSA contracting.

Building Trust and Credibility

Trust is the currency of business in the GSA contracting arena, and credibility is its foundation. Organizations must prioritize transparency, integrity, and reliability in their interactions with clients, partners, and stakeholders. By delivering on promises, honoring commitments, and maintaining the highest ethical standards, organizations can build trust and credibility over time.

Credibility is also built through the consistent demonstration of expertise, authority, and thought leadership. Organizations must provide evidence of their capabilities, achievements, and track record of success in delivering value to clients and stakeholders. By showcasing past performance, client testimonials, and case studies, organizations can bolster their credibility and differentiate themselves in the competitive marketplace.

Collaboration and Partnership

Demonstrating expertise and authority is not just about individual achievements—it's also about leveraging collective knowledge and capabilities through collaboration and partnership. Organizations must seek opportunities to collaborate with industry peers, government agencies, academic institutions, and other stakeholders to address common challenges and drive collective innovation.

By forming strategic partnerships and alliances, organizations can combine complementary strengths, share resources, and amplify their impact within the GSA ecosystem. Collaboration enables organizations to tackle complex problems, explore new opportunities, and achieve outcomes that would be unattainable on their own.

Conclusion

In the competitive and dynamic world of GSA contracting, demonstrating expertise and authority is essential for organizations seeking to establish themselves as trusted partners and leaders in the field. By building domain expertise, cultivating thought leadership, building trust and credibility, and fostering collaboration and partnership, organizations can position themselves for success and achieve enduring excellence in the competitive landscape of government contracting. In prioritizing expertise and authority, organizations can influence outcomes, drive innovation, and make a meaningful impact within the GSA ecosystem.

"Success usually comes to
those who are too busy to be
looking for it."
HENRY DAVID
THOREAU

Law 22

Seize Opportunities Diligently: Identify and seize opportunities within the GSA Multiple Award Schedule promptly and diligently to gain a competitive advantage.

In the realm of General Services Administration (GSA) contracting, opportunities are fleeting, and success favors those who are diligent, proactive, and decisive in their pursuit. Seizing opportunities diligently requires a combination of strategic foresight, readiness to act, and the ability to capitalize on emerging trends and market dynamics within the GSA landscape.

Recognizing Opportunities

The first step in seizing opportunities diligently is the ability to recognize them amidst the noise and complexity of the GSA environment. Organizations must stay attuned to market trends, client needs, and emerging opportunities that align with their capabilities and strategic objectives.

Opportunities may arise in various forms, including requests for proposals (RFPs), solicitations, industry events, networking opportunities, and changes in regulatory frameworks. By maintaining a keen awareness of their environment and actively monitoring developments, organizations can identify opportunities that have the potential to drive growth, innovation, and value creation.

Strategic Evaluation

Not all opportunities are created equal, and organizations must evaluate them strategically to determine their viability, alignment with organizational goals, and potential for success. This involves conducting thorough due diligence, assessing risks and rewards, and analyzing the competitive landscape to gauge the organization's competitive position.

Strategic evaluation also requires organizations to consider factors such as resource availability, capacity, and capability to execute on the opportunity effectively. By weighing these factors carefully, organizations can make informed decisions about which opportunities to pursue and allocate resources accordingly.

Timely Action

Seizing opportunities diligently requires a sense of urgency and readiness to act decisively when opportunities present themselves. Organizations must be agile and responsive, capable of mobilizing resources, assembling cross-functional teams, and developing tailored solutions to address client needs and requirements.

Timely action also involves a commitment to responsiveness and agility in the proposal development and submission process. Organizations must adhere to deadlines, submit high-quality proposals, and engage proactively with clients and stakeholders to demonstrate their commitment and responsiveness.

Continuous Improvement

Seizing opportunities diligently is not a one-time event but an ongoing process of learning, adaptation, and continuous improvement. Organizations must review their performance, gather feedback, and identify lessons learned from past experiences to inform future decision-making and strategy development.

Continuous improvement also involves refining processes, enhancing capabilities, and investing in innovation to stay ahead of the curve and capitalize on emerging opportunities within the GSA landscape. By embracing a mindset of continuous improvement, organizations can adapt to changing circumstances, mitigate risks, and position themselves for sustained success in the competitive environment of government contracting.

Conclusion

In the competitive and dynamic world of GSA contracting, seizing opportunities diligently is essential for organizations seeking to thrive and succeed. By recognizing opportunities, evaluating them strategically, taking timely action, and embracing continuous improvement, organizations can position themselves as leaders in the field and achieve enduring excellence in the pursuit of GSA contracts. In prioritizing diligence and proactive action, organizations can capitalize on opportunities, drive innovation, and create value within the ever-evolving landscape of government contracting.

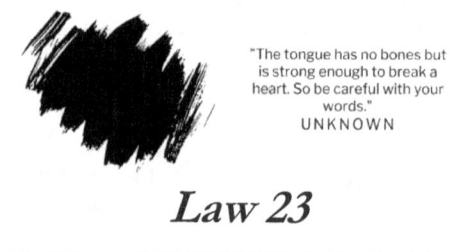

"The tongue has no bones but is strong enough to break a heart. So be careful with your words."
UNKNOWN

Law 23

Exercise Discretion and Tact: Exercise discretion and tact in your interactions with GSA officials, clients, and competitors to maintain positive relationships and avoid unnecessary conflicts.

In the intricate landscape of General Services Administration (GSA) contracting, exercising discretion and tact is essential for navigating complex relationships, maintaining positive interactions, and safeguarding organizational interests. Effective communication, diplomacy, and tactfulness are critical skills that enable organizations to build trust, resolve conflicts, and achieve mutually beneficial outcomes within the GSA ecosystem.

The Importance of Discretion

Discretion involves the ability to make thoughtful and prudent decisions, particularly in sensitive or confidential situations. In the context of GSA contracting, organizations often deal with proprietary information, competitive intelligence, and confidential client data that must be handled with discretion and care.

Exercising discretion entails respecting confidentiality agreements, safeguarding sensitive information, and maintaining the trust and confidence of clients, partners, and stakeholders. Organizations must establish clear policies and protocols for handling confidential information and provide training to employees on the importance of discretion in their interactions.

Tactful Communication

Tactful communication is the art of expressing ideas, opinions, and feedback in a diplomatic and respectful manner. In the competitive and high-stakes environment of GSA contracting, effective communication can mean the difference between success and failure.

Tactful communication involves active listening, empathy, and sensitivity to the perspectives and concerns of others. It requires the ability to deliver constructive feedback, address conflicts, and negotiate differences of opinion in a manner that preserves relationships and fosters collaboration.

Navigating Complex Relationships

GSA contracting often involves navigating complex relationships with multiple stakeholders, including government agencies, clients, partners, and competitors. In these interactions, exercising discretion and tact is essential for building trust, managing expectations, and resolving conflicts amicably.

Organizations must prioritize relationship-building as a strategic imperative, investing time and effort in understanding the needs and preferences of their stakeholders. By demonstrating empathy, respect, and professionalism in their interactions, organizations can cultivate positive relationships that enhance their reputation and credibility within the GSA ecosystem.

Conflict Resolution

Conflicts are inevitable in the competitive environment of GSA contracting, but how organizations handle them can significantly impact their success and reputation. Effective conflict resolution requires a combination of empathy, communication skills, and a commitment to finding mutually acceptable solutions.

Organizations must approach conflicts with a mindset of collaboration and problem-solving, seeking common ground and exploring win-win solutions that address the interests of all parties involved. By fostering a culture of open communication and constructive dialogue, organizations can resolve conflicts effectively and maintain positive relationships with their stakeholders.

Conclusion

In the dynamic and competitive world of GSA contracting, exercising discretion and tact is essential for building trust, fostering positive relationships, and achieving successful outcomes. By prioritizing discretion, tactful communication, and effective conflict resolution, organizations can navigate the complexities of government contracting with professionalism and integrity. In embracing these principles, organizations can build lasting relationships, mitigate risks, and position themselves for sustained success in the competitive landscape of GSA contracting.

"The only limit to our
realization of tomorrow will be
our doubts of today."
FRANKLIN D.
ROOSEVELT

Law 24

Cultivate Resilience: Develop resilience and perseverance to overcome setbacks, challenges, and rejections encountered in the GSA contracting process.

In the challenging and unpredictable terrain of General Services Administration (GSA) contracting, resilience emerges as a critical attribute that separates successful organizations from the rest. Cultivating resilience involves developing the capacity to bounce back from setbacks, adapt to adversity, and thrive in the face of challenges within the dynamic landscape of government contracting.

Understanding Resilience

Resilience is the ability to withstand, recover from, and adapt to adversity, uncertainty, and change. In the context of GSA contracting, resilience enables organizations to navigate through setbacks, rejections, and unexpected challenges without losing sight of their long-term goals and objectives.

Resilient organizations possess a combination of mental toughness, adaptability, and resourcefulness that enables them to persevere in the face of adversity. They view challenges as opportunities for growth and learning, rather than insurmountable obstacles, and approach setbacks with a sense of optimism and determination.

Building Mental Toughness

Mental toughness is a cornerstone of resilience, empowering individuals and organizations to maintain focus, stay motivated, and persevere in the face of adversity. Resilient individuals possess a growth mindset, viewing setbacks and failures as temporary setbacks rather than permanent defeats.

Building mental toughness requires cultivating self-awareness, emotional intelligence, and a positive mindset. Organizations must provide support, encouragement, and resources to help employees develop resilience and cope with stress, uncertainty, and adversity in the workplace.

Adaptability and Flexibility

Adaptability is another key component of resilience, enabling organizations to pivot quickly and adjust their strategies in response to changing circumstances and market dynamics. Resilient organizations are agile and flexible, capable of navigating through uncertainty and capitalizing on emerging opportunities.

Adaptability requires organizations to foster a culture of experimentation, innovation, and continuous improvement. Leaders must encourage creativity, empower employees to take calculated risks, and provide the necessary resources and support to explore new ideas and approaches.

Building a Support Network

Building a support network is essential for cultivating resilience in the competitive environment of GSA contracting. Organizations must foster a sense of community, collaboration, and mutual support among employees, partners, and stakeholders.

A strong support network provides individuals and organizations with the encouragement, guidance, and resources needed to overcome challenges and persevere in the pursuit of their goals. Organizations must invest in building relationships, cultivating partnerships, and fostering a culture of trust and camaraderie within their teams and across the GSA ecosystem.

Conclusion

In the dynamic and competitive world of GSA contracting, cultivating resilience is essential for organizations seeking to thrive and succeed. By building mental toughness, fostering adaptability, and building a strong support network, organizations can navigate through adversity, overcome challenges, and achieve enduring success in the ever-evolving landscape of government contracting. In embracing resilience as a core value, organizations can weather the storms of uncertainty, seize opportunities for growth, and emerge stronger and more resilient than before.

"The only thing that is constant is change."
HERACLITUS

Law 25

Invest in Continuous Learning: Commit to ongoing learning and professional development to stay ahead of the curve and adapt to the evolving landscape of GSA contracting.

In the fast-paced and ever-evolving realm of General Services Administration (GSA) contracting, investing in continuous learning is not just advantageous but imperative for organizations aiming to remain competitive, innovative, and relevant. Continuous learning enables organizations to stay ahead of the curve, adapt to changing market dynamics, and capitalize on emerging opportunities within the GSA landscape.

Embracing Lifelong Learning

Lifelong learning is a mindset—a commitment to ongoing personal and professional development that extends throughout one's career. In the context of GSA contracting, individuals and organizations must embrace a culture of continuous learning to remain agile, adaptable, and responsive to evolving client needs and market trends.

Continuous learning involves seeking out new knowledge, acquiring new skills, and staying abreast of emerging technologies, best practices, and industry trends. It requires a willingness to challenge assumptions, explore new ideas, and push the boundaries of what is possible within the realm of government contracting.

Professional Development Initiatives

Organizations must invest in professional development initiatives that empower employees to expand their skills, deepen their expertise, and enhance their capabilities in GSA contracting. This may involve providing access to training programs, workshops, certifications, and conferences that cover relevant topics such as procurement regulations, contract management, negotiation strategies, and emerging technologies.

Professional development initiatives should be tailored to the specific needs and interests of employees, aligning with organizational goals and priorities. By investing in the growth and development of their workforce, organizations can foster a culture of excellence, innovation, and continuous improvement that drives success in the competitive landscape of government contracting.

Knowledge Sharing and Collaboration

Knowledge sharing and collaboration are essential components of continuous learning within organizations. By creating platforms and opportunities for employees to share insights, expertise, and best practices, organizations can foster a culture of collaboration and collective learning that benefits the entire team.

Knowledge sharing can take many forms, including team meetings, brainstorming sessions, peer-to-peer learning networks, and collaborative projects. Organizations should encourage open communication, constructive feedback, and the exchange of ideas across departments, teams, and levels of the organization.

Staying Abreast of Industry Trends

In the rapidly evolving landscape of GSA contracting, staying abreast of industry trends and market developments is essential for organizations seeking to remain competitive and innovative. Organizations must monitor changes in regulations, policies, and client requirements, as well as emerging technologies and market trends that may impact the GSA landscape.

Staying informed requires a proactive approach to information gathering, including reading industry publications, attending conferences and webinars, participating in industry forums, and networking with peers and thought leaders. By staying abreast of industry trends, organizations can anticipate changes, identify opportunities, and adapt their strategies to stay ahead of the curve in the competitive world of government contracting.

Conclusion

In the competitive and dynamic world of GSA contracting, investing in continuous learning is a strategic imperative for organizations seeking to thrive and succeed. By embracing lifelong learning, investing in professional development initiatives, fostering knowledge sharing and collaboration, and staying abreast of industry trends, organizations can position themselves as leaders in the field and achieve enduring success in the ever-evolving landscape of government contracting. In prioritizing continuous learning, organizations can adapt to change, drive innovation, and create value within the competitive arena of GSA contracting.

"Honesty is the first chapter in
the book of wisdom."

THOMAS JEFFERSON

Law 26

Foster Transparency and Integrity: Maintain transparency in your dealings and adhere to high ethical standards to build trust and credibility with GSA and client stakeholders.

Transparency and integrity serve as cornerstones in the realm of General Services Administration (GSA) contracting, fostering trust, credibility, and sustainable relationships with stakeholders. Organizations that prioritize transparency in their dealings and uphold high ethical standards demonstrate a commitment to accountability and integrity, laying the groundwork for successful partnerships and long-term success.

The Importance of Transparency

Transparency is the foundation upon which trust and credibility are built in the GSA contracting landscape. By providing clear and open communication regarding processes, procedures, and decisions, organizations foster an environment of trust and accountability among GSA officials, clients, partners, and employees.

Transparency involves disclosing relevant information, including pricing structures, contract terms, and performance metrics, to stakeholders in a timely and accessible manner. Organizations must ensure that information is communicated honestly, accurately, and comprehensively, enabling stakeholders to make informed decisions and hold the organization accountable for its actions.

Upholding Ethical Standards

Integrity is non-negotiable in GSA contracting, where ethical conduct is paramount to maintaining the integrity of the procurement process and safeguarding public trust. Organizations must adhere to the highest ethical standards in their interactions with GSA officials, clients, competitors, and partners, avoiding conflicts of interest, bribery, and other unethical practices.

Upholding ethical standards requires a commitment from leadership to foster a culture of integrity and accountability throughout the organization. Organizations must establish clear codes of conduct, policies, and procedures that govern ethical behavior and provide training and support to employees to ensure compliance.

Building Trust and Credibility

Transparency and integrity are instrumental in building trust and credibility with GSA and client stakeholders. By demonstrating a commitment to transparency and ethical conduct, organizations signal their reliability, credibility, and commitment to upholding the public trust.

Building trust and credibility requires consistency, reliability, and a track record of integrity in all dealings with stakeholders. Organizations must deliver on promises, honor commitments, and take responsibility for their actions, earning the trust and confidence of GSA officials, clients, and partners over time.

Nurturing Sustainable Relationships

Transparency and integrity lay the groundwork for sustainable relationships built on trust, respect, and mutual benefit. Organizations that prioritize transparency and integrity foster strong, enduring relationships with GSA officials, clients, and partners, positioning themselves as trusted advisors and reliable partners in the GSA contracting ecosystem.

Nurturing sustainable relationships requires ongoing communication, collaboration, and a shared commitment to transparency and integrity. Organizations must listen to stakeholder feedback, address concerns proactively, and continually demonstrate their commitment to ethical conduct and transparency in all aspects of their operations.

Conclusion

Fostering transparency and integrity is essential for organizations seeking to thrive and succeed in the competitive landscape of GSA contracting. By prioritizing transparency, upholding ethical standards, building trust and credibility, and nurturing sustainable relationships, organizations can position themselves as leaders in the field and achieve enduring success in the dynamic and ever-evolving world of government contracting. In embracing transparency and integrity as guiding principles, organizations can forge strong, lasting partnerships and contribute to the integrity and effectiveness of the GSA contracting process.

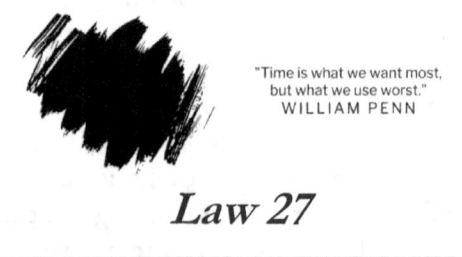

"Time is what we want most, but what we use worst."
WILLIAM PENN

Law 27

Strategically Manage Time and Resources: Effectively allocate time, manpower, and resources to maximize productivity and efficiency in pursuing and fulfilling GSA contracts.

In the intricate realm of General Services Administration (GSA) contracting, strategic management of time and resources is imperative for organizations aiming to maximize productivity, efficiency, and success in pursuing and fulfilling GSA contracts. Effective allocation and utilization of time, manpower, and resources enable organizations to optimize their operations, minimize waste, and achieve their objectives in a competitive and dynamic environment.

Prioritizing Tasks and Objectives

Strategic time and resource management begin with prioritization—identifying key tasks, goals, and objectives that align with organizational priorities and GSA contract requirements. Organizations must establish clear criteria for prioritizing tasks, considering factors such as urgency, importance, and alignment with strategic objectives.

By prioritizing tasks effectively, organizations can focus their time and resources on activities that yield the greatest impact and value in pursuing and fulfilling GSA contracts. This involves setting clear goals, defining measurable outcomes, and aligning activities with broader organizational strategies and objectives.

Optimizing Resource Allocation

Resource allocation is a critical component of strategic management, involving the allocation of manpower, financial resources, and technological assets to support GSA contract activities and initiatives. Organizations must assess their resource needs, capabilities, and constraints to develop a strategic allocation plan that optimizes resource utilization and maximizes efficiency.

Effective resource allocation requires careful planning, forecasting, and monitoring to ensure that resources are allocated efficiently and effectively to support GSA contract requirements and deliverables. Organizations must also be prepared to adapt and reallocate resources as needed in response to changing priorities, market dynamics, and client needs.

Streamlining Workflows and Processes

Streamlining workflows and processes is essential for optimizing productivity and efficiency in pursuing and fulfilling GSA contracts. Organizations must evaluate existing processes, identify bottlenecks and inefficiencies, and implement strategies to streamline workflows and eliminate waste.

This may involve automation of repetitive tasks, standardization of processes, and implementation of best practices to optimize resource utilization and minimize unnecessary delays and errors. By streamlining workflows and processes, organizations can enhance productivity, reduce costs, and improve the overall quality of their GSA contract deliverables.

Embracing Technology and Innovation

Technology and innovation play a pivotal role in strategic resource management, offering opportunities to enhance efficiency, collaboration, and decision-making in GSA contracting activities. Organizations must leverage technological solutions such as project management software, collaboration tools, and data analytics platforms to streamline operations and optimize resource allocation.

Embracing innovation also involves exploring new technologies, methodologies, and best practices that can help organizations improve productivity, enhance performance, and gain a competitive edge in the GSA marketplace. By embracing technology and innovation, organizations can unlock new opportunities for growth, efficiency, and success in pursuing and fulfilling GSA contracts.

Conclusion

Strategic management of time and resources is essential for organizations seeking to thrive and succeed in the competitive landscape of GSA contracting. By prioritizing tasks and objectives, optimizing resource allocation, streamlining workflows and processes, and embracing technology and innovation, organizations can maximize productivity, efficiency, and success in pursuing and fulfilling GSA contracts. In prioritizing strategic resource management, organizations can achieve their goals, fulfill their commitments, and drive sustainable growth and success in the dynamic and ever-evolving world of government contracting.

"Your brand is what other people say about you when you're not in the room."
JEFF BEZOS

Law 28

Cultivate a Strong Brand Identity: Develop a strong brand identity and positioning to differentiate yourself and create a lasting impression in the minds of GSA clients and decision-makers.

In the dynamic and competitive environment of General Services Administration (GSA) contracting, cultivating a strong brand identity is essential for organizations seeking to stand out, differentiate themselves, and create a lasting impression in the minds of GSA clients and decision-makers. A strong brand identity serves as a cornerstone of credibility, trust, and recognition, enabling organizations to build relationships, win contracts, and drive success in the GSA marketplace.

Defining Your Brand Identity

Brand identity encompasses the essence of who you are as an organization—your values, mission, personality, and unique value proposition. Organizations must invest time and effort in defining their brand identity, articulating what sets them apart from competitors and resonates with GSA clients and stakeholders.

Defining your brand identity involves clarifying your organization's core values, vision, and mission statement, as well as identifying key differentiators and competitive advantages. Organizations must also consider their target audience, market positioning, and desired perception in crafting a compelling brand identity that resonates with GSA clients and decision-makers.

Consistency Across Touchpoints

Consistency is key to building a strong brand identity that resonates with GSA clients and stakeholders across various touchpoints and interactions. Organizations must ensure that their brand identity is consistently communicated and reinforced through all channels, including marketing materials, website, social media presence, and client interactions.

Consistency involves maintaining visual elements such as logos, colors, typography, and imagery that reflect the organization's brand identity and values. It also extends to messaging, tone of voice, and communication style, ensuring that all interactions with GSA clients and stakeholders reflect the organization's brand personality and positioning.

Differentiation and Positioning

In the crowded marketplace of GSA contracting, differentiation is essential for organizations seeking to stand out and capture the attention of GSA clients and decision-makers. Organizations must identify and articulate their unique value proposition—the distinctive benefits and advantages they offer compared to competitors.

Differentiation may stem from various factors, including specialized expertise, innovative solutions, exceptional service, or a unique approach to addressing client needs and challenges. By clearly communicating their unique value proposition, organizations can position themselves effectively in the minds of GSA clients and stakeholders and differentiate themselves from competitors.

Building Trust and Credibility

A strong brand identity is synonymous with trust and credibility—qualities that are essential for organizations seeking to win contracts and build lasting relationships in the GSA marketplace. Organizations must uphold their brand promises, deliver on commitments, and consistently demonstrate integrity and reliability in their interactions with GSA clients and stakeholders.

Building trust and credibility requires authenticity, transparency, and a commitment to excellence in all aspects of GSA contracting. Organizations must prioritize client satisfaction, responsiveness, and quality of service to build trust and credibility over time, earning the loyalty and confidence of GSA clients and decision-makers.

Conclusion

Cultivating a strong brand identity is essential for organizations seeking to thrive and succeed in the competitive landscape of GSA contracting. By defining their brand identity, maintaining consistency across touchpoints, differentiating themselves from competitors, and building trust and credibility, organizations can create a powerful brand presence that resonates with GSA clients and decision-makers. In prioritizing brand identity, organizations can establish themselves as trusted partners, win contracts, and drive success in the dynamic and ever-evolving world of government contracting.

"Diversity is the one true thing
we all have in common.
Celebrate it every day."
UNKNOWN

Law 29

Embrace Cultural Sensitivity and Diversity: Respect and embrace cultural diversity and sensitivity in your interactions with GSA officials, clients, and partners to foster inclusive and mutually beneficial relationships.

In the diverse and interconnected world of General Services Administration (GSA) contracting, embracing cultural sensitivity and diversity is paramount for organizations seeking to foster inclusive and mutually beneficial relationships with GSA officials, clients, partners, and stakeholders. Embracing cultural sensitivity and diversity enhances understanding, respect, and collaboration across different cultural backgrounds, promoting innovation, creativity, and success in the GSA marketplace.

Respect for Cultural Differences

Cultural sensitivity begins with a deep respect for cultural differences and an appreciation of the unique perspectives, values, and traditions that individuals from diverse backgrounds bring to the table. Organizations must cultivate an environment of inclusivity, respect, and acceptance, where individuals feel valued and respected regardless of their cultural heritage or background.

Respecting cultural differences involves actively listening, seeking to understand, and embracing diverse viewpoints and experiences. Organizations must create opportunities for open dialogue, cross-cultural communication, and collaboration, fostering a culture of inclusivity and mutual respect within the GSA contracting ecosystem.

Promoting Diversity and Inclusion

Diversity and inclusion are essential for driving innovation, creativity, and success in the GSA marketplace. Organizations must actively promote diversity and inclusion in their workforce, leadership, and business practices, recognizing that diverse perspectives and experiences enrich decision-making, problem-solving, and innovation.

Promoting diversity and inclusion involves implementing policies and initiatives that attract, retain, and empower individuals from diverse backgrounds. Organizations must create a culture of belonging and equity, where all employees feel valued, respected, and empowered to contribute their unique talents and perspectives to the organization's success.

Cultural Competence in Interactions

Cultural competence is the ability to effectively navigate and communicate across different cultural contexts, fostering understanding, trust, and collaboration in GSA contracting relationships. Organizations must invest in cultural competency training and education for employees, equipping them with the knowledge, skills, and awareness needed to navigate diverse cultural landscapes with sensitivity and respect.

Cultural competence involves awareness of cultural norms, communication styles, and practices that may vary across different cultural groups. Organizations must approach interactions with GSA officials, clients, and partners with humility, curiosity, and a willingness to learn, adapting their communication and behavior to foster positive relationships and mutual understanding.

Fostering Inclusive Partnerships

Inclusive partnerships are built on a foundation of trust, respect, and mutual benefit, transcending cultural barriers and fostering collaboration and innovation in GSA contracting relationships. Organizations must seek out diverse perspectives and experiences in their partnerships, recognizing the value of inclusivity in driving success and sustainability.

Fostering inclusive partnerships requires a commitment to equitable opportunities, shared decision-making, and transparent communication among all stakeholders. Organizations must create environments where diversity is celebrated, differences are embraced, and individuals are empowered to contribute their unique talents and perspectives to collaborative endeavors.

Conclusion

Embracing cultural sensitivity and diversity is essential for organizations seeking to thrive and succeed in the diverse and interconnected world of GSA contracting. By respecting cultural differences, promoting diversity and inclusion, fostering cultural competence in interactions, and fostering inclusive partnerships, organizations can build strong, resilient relationships that drive innovation, creativity, and success in the GSA marketplace. In prioritizing cultural sensitivity and diversity, organizations can create inclusive environments where all individuals feel valued, respected, and empowered to contribute their diverse perspectives and talents to the pursuit of excellence in government contracting.

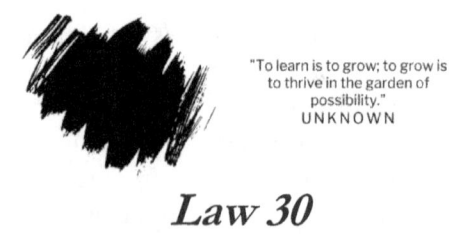

"To learn is to grow; to grow is to thrive in the garden of possibility."
UNKNOWN

Law 30

Stay Abreast of Compliance Requirements: Stay updated on regulatory and compliance requirements governing GSA

contracts to ensure adherence and mitigate the risk of penalties or contract disputes.

In the complex and regulated landscape of General Services Administration (GSA) contracting, staying updated on regulatory and compliance requirements is crucial for organizations to ensure adherence and mitigate the risk of penalties or contract disputes. Compliance requirements govern various aspects of GSA contracts, including procurement regulations, contract terms, reporting obligations, and ethical standards. Organizations must prioritize compliance as a foundational element of their operations to maintain trust, credibility, and legal integrity in the GSA marketplace.

Understanding Regulatory Frameworks

The regulatory framework surrounding GSA contracting is multifaceted and subject to change, encompassing Federal Acquisition Regulations (FAR), agency-specific guidelines, procurement policies, and ethical standards. Organizations must have a comprehensive understanding of the regulatory landscape governing GSA contracts to navigate compliance requirements effectively.

Understanding regulatory frameworks involves conducting thorough research, engaging with legal counsel, and staying informed about updates, amendments, and interpretations of relevant regulations. Organizations must prioritize compliance as a strategic imperative, integrating compliance considerations into their policies, procedures, and decision-making processes.

Adhering to Contract Terms

GSA contracts are governed by specific terms and conditions outlined in the contract documents, including pricing schedules, performance metrics, delivery schedules, and reporting requirements. Organizations must familiarize themselves with the terms of their GSA contracts and ensure strict adherence to contractual obligations to avoid penalties, disputes, or contract terminations.

Adhering to contract terms requires effective contract management processes, including document retention, performance tracking, and reporting mechanisms. Organizations must establish internal controls and oversight mechanisms to monitor compliance with contract terms and address any deviations or discrepancies proactively.

Mitigating Compliance Risks

Compliance risks in GSA contracting can arise from various sources, including regulatory changes, contractual breaches, conflicts of interest, and ethical lapses. Organizations must proactively identify, assess, and mitigate compliance risks to protect their business interests and uphold legal and ethical standards.

Mitigating compliance risks involves conducting risk assessments, implementing internal controls, and establishing monitoring mechanisms to detect and prevent compliance violations. Organizations must provide training and guidance to employees on compliance requirements, ethical standards, and reporting obligations to promote a culture of integrity and accountability.

Engaging in Continuous Monitoring and Improvement

Compliance in GSA contracting is an ongoing process that requires continuous monitoring, evaluation, and improvement. Organizations must establish mechanisms for monitoring compliance performance, conducting internal audits, and addressing identified deficiencies or areas for improvement.

Engaging in continuous monitoring and improvement involves soliciting feedback from stakeholders, analyzing compliance data, and implementing corrective actions to enhance compliance effectiveness. Organizations must stay vigilant against emerging compliance risks and proactively adapt their strategies and processes to address evolving regulatory requirements and industry best practices.

Conclusion

Staying abreast of compliance requirements is essential for organizations seeking to maintain trust, credibility, and legal integrity in the competitive landscape of GSA contracting. By understanding regulatory frameworks, adhering to contract terms, mitigating compliance risks, and engaging in continuous monitoring and improvement, organizations can uphold ethical standards, mitigate legal liabilities, and position themselves for success in the dynamic and regulated environment of government contracting. In prioritizing compliance, organizations demonstrate their commitment to integrity, transparency, and responsible stewardship of public resources in the pursuit of excellence in GSA contracting.

"Without big data, you are blind and deaf and in the middle of a freeway."
GEOFFREY MOORE

Law 31

Harness the Power of Data and Analytics: Leverage data analytics and business intelligence tools to gain actionable insights and inform strategic decision-making in pursuing and managing GSA contracts.

In the increasingly data-driven landscape of General Services Administration (GSA) contracting, harnessing the power of data and analytics is essential for organizations seeking to gain actionable insights and inform strategic decision-making. Data and analytics provide valuable intelligence that enables organizations to optimize performance, identify opportunities, mitigate risks, and drive success in the competitive marketplace of GSA contracting.

Data Collection and Aggregation

The first step in harnessing the power of data and analytics is collecting and aggregating relevant data from various sources within the organization and the GSA ecosystem. Data sources may include contract performance metrics, financial records, client feedback, market trends, and competitive intelligence.

Organizations must establish robust data collection mechanisms and leverage technology solutions to aggregate, consolidate, and organize data effectively. This may involve implementing data management systems, leveraging cloud-based platforms, and integrating data from disparate sources to create a comprehensive data repository.

Data Analysis and Visualization

Once data is collected and aggregated, organizations must analyze and visualize the data to extract actionable insights and trends. Data analysis involves applying statistical techniques, data mining algorithms, and machine learning models to uncover patterns, correlations, and anomalies within the data.

Data visualization plays a crucial role in transforming complex datasets into intuitive and actionable visual representations, such as charts, graphs, dashboards, and heatmaps. Visualization tools enable stakeholders to explore data interactively, identify trends, and make informed decisions based on data-driven insights.

Strategic Decision-Making

Data and analytics empower organizations to make strategic decisions informed by evidence and insights rather than intuition or guesswork. By leveraging data-driven insights, organizations can optimize resource allocation, identify growth opportunities, and mitigate risks in GSA contracting activities.

Strategic decision-making based on data and analytics involves evaluating alternative scenarios, assessing potential outcomes, and quantifying the impact of strategic initiatives on key performance indicators. Organizations must involve stakeholders from across the organization in the decision-making process, leveraging data-driven insights to align priorities and drive consensus.

Performance Monitoring and Optimization

Data and analytics enable organizations to monitor performance, track progress, and optimize operations in real-time. By establishing key performance indicators (KPIs) and performance benchmarks, organizations can measure the effectiveness of their GSA contracting activities and identify areas for improvement.

Performance monitoring involves regularly evaluating performance against established KPIs, analyzing trends and deviations, and identifying opportunities for optimization and efficiency gains. Organizations must leverage data and analytics to iterate on their strategies, refine their approaches, and continuously improve performance in GSA contracting activities.

Conclusion

Harnessing the power of data and analytics is essential for organizations seeking to thrive and succeed in the competitive landscape of GSA contracting. By collecting and aggregating relevant data, analyzing and visualizing data-driven insights, making strategic decisions informed by evidence, and monitoring performance for optimization, organizations can leverage data as a strategic asset to drive success in government contracting. In prioritizing data and analytics, organizations demonstrate their commitment to innovation, agility, and excellence in the pursuit of growth and success in the dynamic world of GSA contracting.

"Price is what you pay. Value is
what you get."
WARREN BUFFETT

Law 32

Emphasize Value Proposition Over Price: Focus on communicating the value and benefits of your offerings rather than solely competing on price to win GSA contracts and maintain profitability.

In the intricate realm of General Services Administration (GSA) contracting, emphasizing the value proposition over price is paramount for organizations aiming to secure contracts and maintain profitability in a competitive marketplace. While price plays a crucial role in decision-making, organizations that prioritize and effectively communicate their value proposition can differentiate themselves, build strong relationships, and achieve long-term success in GSA contracting.

Understanding the Value Proposition

The value proposition encompasses the unique benefits, solutions, and advantages that organizations offer to GSA clients and stakeholders. It goes beyond price considerations and encompasses factors such as quality, reliability, innovation, expertise, and customer service.

Organizations must understand their value proposition thoroughly, articulating how their offerings address client needs, solve pain points, and deliver tangible benefits and outcomes. By focusing on the value they provide rather than simply competing on price, organizations can position themselves as trusted partners and solution providers in GSA contracting.

Aligning with Client Needs

Successful GSA contracting hinges on the ability to align with client needs and priorities effectively. Organizations must invest time and effort in understanding client requirements, challenges, and objectives, tailoring their value proposition to address specific client pain points and deliver maximum value.

By demonstrating a deep understanding of client needs and articulating how their solutions can address those needs effectively, organizations can differentiate themselves from competitors and position themselves as valuable partners in GSA contracting initiatives.

Communicating Differentiators Effectively

Effective communication is essential for conveying the value proposition to GSA clients and stakeholders convincingly. Organizations must develop clear and compelling messaging that highlights their unique differentiators, competitive advantages, and value-added services in a concise and persuasive manner.

Communication strategies may include case studies, testimonials, demonstrations, and presentations that showcase the organization's capabilities, track record, and success stories in GSA contracting. By leveraging various communication channels and platforms, organizations can amplify their message and resonate with GSA clients and decision-makers effectively.

Demonstrating Return on Investment

GSA clients are often focused on achieving measurable results and return on investment (ROI) from contracting initiatives. Organizations must demonstrate the potential ROI of their solutions by quantifying the benefits, cost savings, and efficiencies that clients can expect to realize by partnering with them.

This may involve conducting cost-benefit analyses, ROI calculations, and total cost of ownership assessments to illustrate the financial impact of implementing the organization's solutions. By providing concrete evidence of the value they offer, organizations can instill confidence and trust in GSA clients and stakeholders and justify premium pricing based on the expected return on investment.

Conclusion

Emphasizing the value proposition over price is essential for organizations seeking to thrive and succeed in GSA contracting. By understanding their value proposition, aligning with client needs, communicating differentiators effectively, and demonstrating return on investment, organizations can differentiate themselves, build strong relationships, and achieve long-term success in the competitive landscape of government contracting. In prioritizing the value proposition, organizations can position themselves as trusted partners and solution providers, driving value and innovation in GSA contracting initiatives.

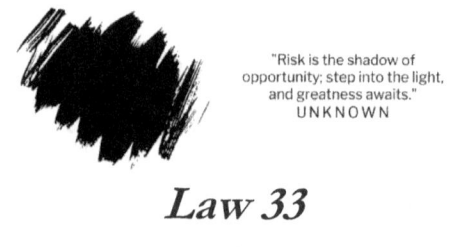

"Risk is the shadow of opportunity; step into the light, and greatness awaits."
UNKNOWN

Law 33

Develop a Robust Risk Management Framework: Establish a comprehensive risk management framework to identify, assess, mitigate, and monitor risks associated with GSA contracts proactively.

In the dynamic and complex environment of General Services Administration (GSA) contracting, developing a robust risk management framework is essential for organizations to identify, assess, mitigate, and monitor risks effectively. GSA contracts are subject to various risks, including regulatory changes, market fluctuations, contractual disputes, and operational challenges. By proactively managing risks, organizations can safeguard their business interests, protect against potential losses, and enhance their resilience in the GSA marketplace.

Identifying Risks

The first step in developing a robust risk management framework is to identify potential risks that may impact GSA contracting activities. Risks can arise from internal and external factors, including regulatory requirements, market conditions, financial constraints, and technological vulnerabilities.

Organizations must conduct comprehensive risk assessments to identify and categorize risks based on their likelihood and potential impact on GSA contracts. This may involve engaging stakeholders from across the organization, analyzing historical data, and leveraging industry benchmarks and best practices to identify emerging risks and trends.

Assessing Risk Exposure

Once risks are identified, organizations must assess their exposure to each risk and prioritize them based on their significance and potential consequences. Risk assessment involves evaluating the likelihood of occurrence and the potential impact of each risk on GSA contracting activities, financial performance, and strategic objectives.

Organizations must consider both qualitative and quantitative factors when assessing risk exposure, including financial impact, operational disruption, reputational damage, and regulatory compliance. By quantifying risk exposure and prioritizing risks based on their severity, organizations can allocate resources and focus their efforts on mitigating the most critical risks.

Mitigating Risks

Risk mitigation involves implementing strategies and controls to reduce the likelihood and impact of identified risks on GSA contracting activities. Mitigation strategies may vary depending on the nature of the risk and the organization's risk tolerance and capabilities.

Mitigation strategies may include implementing internal controls, establishing contingency plans, diversifying supplier relationships, securing insurance coverage, and developing alternative sourcing strategies. Organizations must implement a combination of preventive, detective, and corrective controls to mitigate risks effectively and enhance their resilience in the face of uncertainty.

Monitoring and Reviewing Risks

Risk management is an ongoing process that requires continuous monitoring, review, and adaptation to changing conditions and emerging threats. Organizations must establish mechanisms for monitoring risk indicators, tracking risk events, and assessing the effectiveness of risk mitigation measures.

Regular risk reviews and assessments enable organizations to identify new risks, evaluate the effectiveness of existing controls, and adjust their risk management strategies accordingly. By maintaining vigilance and responsiveness to changing risk dynamics, organizations can adapt proactively to mitigate emerging threats and capitalize on new opportunities in the GSA marketplace.

Conclusion

Developing a robust risk management framework is essential for organizations seeking to thrive and succeed in the competitive landscape of GSA contracting. By identifying risks, assessing risk exposure, mitigating risks, and monitoring and reviewing risks continuously, organizations can enhance their resilience, protect their business interests, and maintain their competitive advantage in the dynamic and uncertain environment of government contracting. In prioritizing risk management, organizations demonstrate their commitment to proactive stewardship, sound governance, and sustainable growth in the GSA marketplace.

"The first step toward success is taken when you refuse to be a captive of the environment in which you first find yourself."
MARK CAINE

Law 34

Cultivate a Culture of Compliance: Instill a culture of compliance and accountability within your organization to uphold GSA contract terms, regulations, and ethical standards rigorously.

In the intricate landscape of General Services Administration (GSA) contracting, cultivating a culture of compliance is paramount for organizations to uphold ethical standards, mitigate legal risks, and maintain trust and credibility with clients and stakeholders. A culture of compliance goes beyond mere adherence to rules and regulations; it embodies a commitment to integrity, transparency, and accountability in all aspects of GSA contracting activities.

Setting the Tone from the Top

Cultivating a culture of compliance begins with leadership commitment and setting the tone from the top. Leaders within the organization must champion ethical behavior, reinforce the importance of compliance, and lead by example in upholding the organization's values and principles.

Leadership commitment to compliance is demonstrated through clear communication of expectations, allocation of resources for compliance initiatives, and accountability for adherence to ethical standards. Leaders must foster an environment where ethical conduct is celebrated, rewarded, and ingrained into the organizational fabric.

Providing Training and Education

Effective compliance requires a well-informed workforce equipped with the knowledge and skills to navigate complex regulatory landscapes and ethical dilemmas. Organizations must invest in comprehensive training and education programs to raise awareness of compliance requirements and empower employees to make ethical decisions.

Compliance training may cover a range of topics, including regulatory requirements, company policies and procedures, conflict of interest guidelines, and reporting mechanisms for potential violations. Training programs should be tailored to the specific needs and roles of employees involved in GSA contracting activities, emphasizing practical scenarios and case studies relevant to their responsibilities.

Establishing Clear Policies and Procedures

Clear and comprehensive policies and procedures serve as the foundation of a culture of compliance, providing employees with guidance on expected behaviors and actions in GSA contracting activities. Organizations must develop and communicate policies that align with regulatory requirements, industry standards, and organizational values.

Policies and procedures should address key areas of compliance, including procurement integrity, conflicts of interest, data privacy, anti-corruption, and recordkeeping. They should be written in clear and accessible language, regularly updated to reflect changes in regulations or organizational practices, and enforced consistently across the organization.

Encouraging Reporting and Whistleblowing

An essential aspect of a culture of compliance is the encouragement of reporting and whistleblowing mechanisms that empower employees to raise concerns about potential compliance violations without fear of retaliation. Organizations must establish confidential reporting channels and procedures for employees to report suspected violations or unethical behavior.

Encouraging reporting requires fostering a safe and supportive environment where employees feel comfortable speaking up and raising concerns. Organizations must take reports seriously, conduct thorough investigations, and take appropriate corrective action in response to substantiated allegations of non-compliance.

Conclusion

Cultivating a culture of compliance is essential for organizations seeking to thrive and succeed in the competitive landscape of GSA contracting. By setting the tone from the top, providing training and education, establishing clear policies and procedures, and encouraging reporting and whistleblowing, organizations can create an environment where ethical conduct is valued, promoted, and rewarded. In prioritizing a culture of compliance, organizations demonstrate their commitment to integrity, transparency, and responsible stewardship in the pursuit of excellence in government contracting.

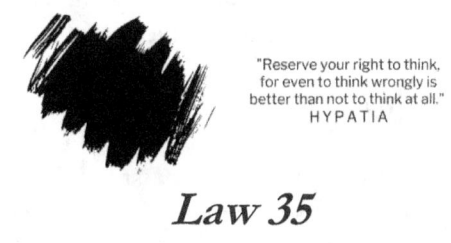

"Reserve your right to think,
for even to think wrongly is
better than not to think at all."
HYPATIA

Law 35

Build Strategic Reserves and Contingencies: Maintain strategic reserves and contingencies to mitigate unforeseen

risks, disruptions, and fluctuations in GSA contract demand or market conditions.

In the ever-evolving environment of General Services Administration (GSA) contracting, building strategic reserves and contingencies is vital for organizations to mitigate risks, adapt to uncertainties, and ensure resilience in the face of challenges. Strategic reserves and contingencies provide organizations with the flexibility and resources needed to respond effectively to unforeseen events, fluctuations in demand, and disruptions in the GSA marketplace.

Understanding Strategic Reserves

Strategic reserves refer to resources, funds, or assets that organizations set aside or maintain as a buffer against potential risks and uncertainties in GSA contracting activities. These reserves may include financial reserves, inventory stockpiles, capacity buffers, or contingency funds that organizations can deploy when needed to address emergent challenges or opportunities.

Strategic reserves enable organizations to maintain operational continuity, capitalize on opportunities, and navigate disruptions without jeopardizing their core business activities or financial stability. By strategically allocating resources to reserves, organizations can enhance their agility and competitiveness in the dynamic landscape of government contracting.

Identifying Contingencies

Contingencies are predefined plans or strategies that organizations develop to address specific risks or scenarios that may arise during the course of GSA contracting activities. Contingencies help organizations anticipate potential challenges, mitigate negative impacts, and capitalize on opportunities in a timely and effective manner.

Contingencies may include alternative sourcing options, backup suppliers, emergency response protocols, crisis management plans, or workforce mobilization strategies. Organizations must identify key risks and vulnerabilities in GSA contracting activities and develop contingency plans tailored to mitigate those risks and ensure business continuity.

Allocating Resources Wisely

Effective management of strategic reserves and contingencies requires prudent allocation of resources, balancing the need for risk mitigation with operational efficiency and financial sustainability. Organizations must assess their risk appetite, financial capacity, and strategic priorities when allocating resources to reserves and contingencies.

Resource allocation decisions should be informed by comprehensive risk assessments, scenario planning exercises, and sensitivity analyses that identify potential impacts on GSA contracting activities. Organizations must prioritize investments in strategic reserves and contingencies that offer the greatest value in terms of risk reduction, opportunity capture, and long-term resilience.

Maintaining Flexibility and Adaptability

Strategic reserves and contingencies provide organizations with the flexibility and adaptability needed to respond to changing market dynamics, regulatory requirements, and client demands in GSA contracting. Organizations must regularly review and update their reserves and contingencies based on evolving risk profiles, emerging threats, and lessons learned from past experiences.

Maintaining flexibility and adaptability requires a proactive approach to risk management, continuous monitoring of key indicators, and regular reassessment of contingency plans. Organizations must remain agile and responsive to emerging challenges and opportunities, adjusting their strategies and resource allocations as needed to stay ahead of the curve in the competitive landscape of government contracting.

Conclusion

Building strategic reserves and contingencies is essential for organizations seeking to thrive and succeed in the dynamic and uncertain environment of GSA contracting. By understanding strategic reserves, identifying contingencies, allocating resources wisely, and maintaining flexibility and adaptability, organizations can mitigate risks, capitalize on opportunities, and ensure resilience in the face of challenges. In prioritizing strategic reserves and contingencies, organizations demonstrate their commitment to proactive risk management, strategic foresight, and sustainable growth in government contracting.

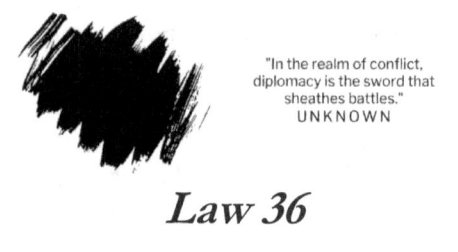

"In the realm of conflict, diplomacy is the sword that sheathes battles."
UNKNOWN

Law 36

Exercise Diplomacy in Disputes and Conflicts: Approach disputes and conflicts with diplomacy, tact, and a commitment to finding mutually acceptable resolutions to preserve relationships and minimize disruptions to GSA contracts.

In the intricate landscape of General Services Administration (GSA) contracting, exercising diplomacy in disputes and conflicts is essential for organizations to preserve relationships, minimize disruptions, and foster productive collaboration with GSA officials, clients, subcontractors, and partners. Disputes and conflicts are inherent in the complex nature of government contracting, arising from divergent interests, competing priorities, and misunderstandings. By approaching disputes with diplomacy, organizations can navigate conflicts effectively, find mutually acceptable resolutions, and maintain positive relationships in the GSA marketplace.

Maintaining Open Lines of Communication

Open and transparent communication is the cornerstone of diplomacy in resolving disputes and conflicts in GSA contracting. Organizations must establish and maintain open lines of communication with all parties involved, facilitating dialogue, understanding perspectives, and seeking common ground for resolution.

Effective communication involves active listening, empathy, and the willingness to consider alternative viewpoints. Organizations must create opportunities for constructive dialogue, engage in meaningful discussions, and work collaboratively to address concerns and find mutually beneficial solutions to disputes and conflicts.

Seeking Common Ground and Compromise

In resolving disputes and conflicts, organizations must seek common ground and explore avenues for compromise that address the interests and concerns of all parties involved. Diplomacy involves finding creative solutions and compromises that balance competing priorities, preserve relationships, and uphold the integrity of GSA contracts.

Organizations must approach negotiations with a spirit of collaboration and flexibility, focusing on shared objectives and the long-term interests of all stakeholders. By demonstrating a willingness to compromise and find win-win solutions, organizations can build trust, foster goodwill, and resolve disputes amicably in the GSA marketplace.

Emphasizing Problem-Solving and Solutions-Oriented Approaches

Diplomacy in disputes and conflicts requires a problem-solving mindset and a solutions-oriented approach to resolution. Organizations must focus on identifying underlying issues, exploring root causes, and developing practical solutions that address the core concerns of all parties involved.

Problem-solving involves analyzing issues objectively, brainstorming creative solutions, and evaluating the potential impact of proposed resolutions on GSA contracting activities. Organizations must engage in collaborative problem-solving processes that encourage innovative thinking, consensus-building, and constructive dialogue among stakeholders.

Maintaining Professionalism and Respect

Maintaining professionalism and respect is paramount in exercising diplomacy in disputes and conflicts in GSA contracting. Organizations must conduct themselves with integrity, civility, and respect for all parties involved, regardless of differences or disagreements.

Professionalism involves refraining from personal attacks, inflammatory language, or adversarial behavior that may escalate tensions and undermine trust. Organizations must uphold ethical standards, adhere to contractual obligations, and conduct negotiations with dignity, professionalism, and respect for the dignity and autonomy of all parties involved.

Conclusion

Exercising diplomacy in disputes and conflicts is essential for organizations seeking to navigate the complexities of GSA contracting successfully. By maintaining open lines of communication, seeking common ground and compromise, emphasizing problem-solving and solutions-oriented approaches, and maintaining professionalism and respect, organizations can resolve disputes amicably, preserve relationships, and foster a collaborative and constructive environment in the GSA market-place. In prioritizing diplomacy, organizations demonstrate their commitment to integrity, collaboration, and conflict resolution in the pursuit of excellence in government contracting.

"Continuous improvement is better than delayed perfection."
MARK TWAIN

Law 37

Continuously Evaluate and Improve Processes: Continuously evaluate and optimize your internal processes, workflows, and systems to streamline operations and enhance efficiency in managing GSA contracts.

In the dynamic landscape of General Services Administration (GSA) contracting, continuous evaluation and improvement of processes are essential for organizations to optimize efficiency, enhance effectiveness, and adapt to evolving requirements. GSA contracts involve complex procedures, stringent regulations, and diverse stakeholders, necessitating streamlined and agile processes to navigate successfully. By embracing a culture of continuous improvement, organizations can identify inefficiencies, address bottlenecks, and drive innovation in GSA contracting activities.

Embracing a Culture of Continuous Improvement

Continuous improvement is more than just a methodology; it is a mindset that permeates throughout the organization, driving ongoing efforts to enhance processes, workflows, and outcomes. Organizations must cultivate a culture that values innovation, feedback, and learning, encouraging employees at all levels to contribute ideas for improvement and actively participate in process refinement initiatives.

Leadership plays a crucial role in promoting a culture of continuous improvement, providing the necessary resources, support, and encouragement for employees to experiment, innovate, and challenge the status quo. By fostering an environment where continuous learning and improvement are celebrated, organizations can empower employees to drive positive change and innovation in GSA contracting activities.

Conducting Regular Process Reviews and Assessments

Effective process improvement begins with regular reviews and assessments of existing processes to identify areas for optimization and enhancement. Organizations must establish mechanisms for evaluating process performance, soliciting feedback from stakeholders, and benchmarking against industry best practices and standards.

Process reviews may involve conducting process mapping exercises, value stream analyses, or root cause analyses to identify inefficiencies, redundancies, or gaps in GSA contracting workflows. By systematically evaluating process performance and identifying opportunities for improvement, organizations can streamline operations, reduce cycle times, and enhance overall efficiency in GSA contracting activities.

Implementing Lean and Agile Methodologies

Lean and agile methodologies offer valuable frameworks for driving process improvement and optimization in GSA contracting. Lean principles emphasize the elimination of waste, standardization of processes, and continuous flow of value to customers. Agile methodologies prioritize flexibility, responsiveness, and iterative development, enabling organizations to adapt quickly to changing requirements and stakeholder needs.

Organizations must leverage lean and agile principles to streamline GSA contracting processes, eliminate non-value-added activities, and enhance responsiveness to client demands. This may involve implementing agile project management methodologies, adopting lean process improvement techniques, and empowering cross-functional teams to collaborate and innovate in GSA contracting initiatives.

Harnessing Technology and Automation

Technology and automation play a pivotal role in driving process improvement and efficiency gains in GSA contracting activities. Organizations must leverage technology solutions, such as contract management systems, workflow automation tools, and data analytics platforms, to streamline processes, reduce manual intervention, and enhance decision-making capabilities.

Technology enables organizations to automate repetitive tasks, standardize workflows, and capture data insights that inform strategic decision-making and process optimization efforts. By harnessing the power of technology, organizations can improve accuracy, reduce cycle times, and enhance overall agility and competitiveness in the GSA marketplace.

Conclusion

Continuous evaluation and improvement of processes are essential for organizations seeking to thrive and succeed in the competitive landscape of GSA contracting. By embracing a culture of continuous improvement, conducting regular process reviews and assessments, implementing lean and agile methodologies, and harnessing technology and automation, organizations can optimize efficiency, enhance effectiveness, and adapt to evolving requirements in GSA contracting activities. In prioritizing continuous improvement, organizations demonstrate their commitment to excellence, innovation, and agility in the pursuit of success in government contracting.

"The secret of business is to know something that nobody else knows."
ARISTOTLE ONASSIS

Law 38

Develop a Robust Competitive Intelligence Strategy: Invest in gathering and analyzing competitive intelligence to identify emerging trends, opportunities, and threats in the GSA marketplace and adjust your strategies accordingly.

In the dynamic and competitive environment of General Services Administration (GSA) contracting, developing a robust competitive intelligence strategy is paramount for organizations to gain insights, anticipate market trends, and make informed decisions. Competitive intelligence encompasses the systematic gathering, analysis, and interpretation of information about competitors, market dynamics, and emerging trends in the GSA marketplace. By leveraging competitive intelligence effectively, organizations can identify opportunities, mitigate threats, and gain a competitive edge in pursuing and managing GSA contracts.

Understanding the Competitive Landscape

The first step in developing a competitive intelligence strategy is to understand the competitive landscape within the GSA marketplace. Organizations must identify key competitors, assess their strengths, weaknesses, capabilities, and market positioning, and analyze their strategies and tactics in pursuing GSA contracts.

Competitive analysis involves gathering information about competitor offerings, pricing strategies, contract wins and losses, past performance evaluations, and client relationships. By understanding the competitive landscape, organizations can identify areas of differentiation, assess market dynamics, and develop strategies to capitalize on opportunities and mitigate threats.

Gathering Actionable Intelligence

Effective competitive intelligence requires the systematic gathering of actionable intelligence from various internal and external sources. Organizations must leverage a combination of primary and secondary research methods to collect information about competitors, market trends, client preferences, and regulatory developments.

Primary research methods may include conducting interviews, surveys, and focus groups with clients, industry experts, and key stakeholders. Secondary research methods involve analyzing publicly available information, industry reports, news articles, and social media channels to gather insights about competitor activities and market trends.

Analyzing and Interpreting Insights

Once information is gathered, organizations must analyze and interpret insights to extract actionable intelligence that informs strategic decision-making. Competitive analysis involves identifying patterns, trends, and emerging issues in the GSA marketplace, and assessing their potential impact on organizational objectives and performance.

Data analytics and business intelligence tools can be leveraged to analyze large datasets, identify correlations, and generate actionable insights. Organizations must develop analytical capabilities to interpret insights effectively, assess competitive threats and opportunities, and develop data-driven strategies to gain a competitive advantage in GSA contracting activities.

Disseminating Insights and Driving Action

The final step in the competitive intelligence process is disseminating insights and driving action across the organization. Organizations must communicate findings and recommendations to key stakeholders, including senior leadership, business development teams, and project managers, to inform decision-making and strategic planning processes.

Effective dissemination of competitive intelligence involves presenting insights in a clear, concise, and actionable manner, tailored to the needs and preferences of different stakeholders. Organizations must foster a culture of data-driven decision-making, encourage collaboration and knowledge sharing, and empower employees to take proactive steps based on competitive insights to achieve organizational goals.

Conclusion

Developing a robust competitive intelligence strategy is essential for organizations seeking to thrive and succeed in the competitive landscape of GSA contracting. By understanding the competitive landscape, gathering actionable intelligence, analyzing and interpreting insights, and disseminating findings effectively, organizations can gain a competitive edge, identify growth opportunities, and mitigate risks in pursuing and managing GSA contracts. In prioritizing competitive intelligence, organizations demonstrate their commitment to strategic foresight, informed decision-making, and sustainable growth in government contracting.

"Change is the law of life. And those who look only to the past or present are certain to miss the future."
JOHN F. KENNEDY

Law 39

Anticipate and Adapt to Regulatory Changes: Anticipate and adapt to changes in GSA regulations, policies, and procurement practices to proactively position your organization for compliance and competitive advantage.

In the intricate world of General Services Administration (GSA) contracting, anticipating and adapting to regulatory changes are essential for organizations to ensure compliance, mitigate risks, and maintain competitiveness. GSA contracts are subject to a myriad of regulations, policies, and guidelines that govern procurement processes, contract administration, and vendor responsibilities. By staying abreast of regulatory developments and proactively adjusting strategies and practices, organizations can navigate regulatory complexities effectively and position themselves for success in the GSA marketplace.

Monitoring Regulatory Landscape

The first step in anticipating regulatory changes is to monitor the regulatory landscape continuously. Organizations must stay informed about updates to GSA regulations, policies, and procurement practices issued by regulatory agencies such as GSA, Office of Management and Budget (OMB), and other relevant authorities.

Monitoring the regulatory landscape involves tracking proposed rulemakings, legislative initiatives, executive orders, and guidance documents that may impact GSA contracting activities. Organizations must establish mechanisms for receiving regulatory updates, such as subscribing to government newsletters, participating in industry forums, and leveraging legal and compliance resources.

Assessing Impact and Implications

Upon identifying regulatory changes, organizations must assess their potential impact and implications on GSA contracts, business operations, and compliance obligations. This involves conducting thorough reviews and analyses of regulatory updates to understand their scope, requirements, and timelines for implementation.

Organizations must evaluate how regulatory changes may affect contract performance, pricing strategies, subcontractor relationships, reporting obligations, and other aspects of GSA contracting activities. By assessing the impact and implications of regulatory changes proactively, organizations can identify areas of vulnerability and develop strategies to address compliance gaps and mitigate risks effectively.

Updating Policies and Procedures

Adapting to regulatory changes requires organizations to update their policies, procedures, and internal controls to ensure alignment with new requirements and expectations. Organizations must review existing policies and procedures governing GSA contracting activities and revise them as necessary to reflect regulatory updates and compliance obligations.

Updating policies and procedures may involve revising contract templates, modifying pricing methodologies, enhancing compliance monitoring processes, and implementing new reporting requirements. Organizations must communicate changes effectively to relevant stakeholders, provide training and guidance on updated policies, and monitor adherence to new procedures to ensure compliance with regulatory requirements.

Engaging with Regulatory Authorities

Engaging with regulatory authorities and industry stakeholders is essential for organizations to gain clarity on regulatory changes, seek guidance on compliance matters, and advocate for their interests in the regulatory process. Organizations must establish proactive channels of communication with regulatory agencies, trade associations, and industry groups to stay informed about regulatory developments and participate in policy discussions.

Engaging with regulatory authorities may involve attending public hearings, submitting comments on proposed regulations, and participating in industry working groups and advisory committees. By actively engaging with regulatory authorities, organizations can influence regulatory outcomes, address concerns, and advocate for policies that support a fair and competitive GSA marketplace.

Conclusion

Anticipating and adapting to regulatory changes are critical imperatives for organizations operating in the dynamic and evolving landscape of GSA contracting. By monitoring the regulatory landscape, assessing the impact and implications of regulatory changes, updating policies and procedures, and engaging with regulatory authorities, organizations can navigate regulatory complexities effectively and ensure compliance with evolving requirements. In prioritizing regulatory agility, organizations demonstrate their commitment to integrity, accountability, and excellence in government contracting, positioning themselves for success in a rapidly changing regulatory environment.

"The customer's perception is
your reality."
KATE ZABRISKIE

Law 40

Foster a Customer-Centric Mindset: Prioritize customer satisfaction and responsiveness to client needs and feedback to cultivate strong, enduring relationships and secure repeat business under GSA contracts.

In the realm of General Services Administration (GSA) contracting, fostering a customer-centric mindset is crucial for organizations to cultivate strong, enduring relationships with GSA officials and clients. A customer-centric approach prioritizes understanding client needs, delivering value-added solutions, and providing exceptional service throughout the contracting lifecycle. By placing the customer at the center of their operations, organizations can enhance satisfaction, loyalty, and repeat business under GSA contracts.

Understanding Client Needs and Expectations

The foundation of a customer-centric mindset lies in understanding the unique needs, preferences, and challenges of GSA officials and clients. Organizations must invest time and resources in gathering insights into client requirements, mission objectives, and performance expectations to tailor their offerings and service delivery accordingly.

Understanding client needs involves conducting thorough needs assessments, engaging in active dialogue with clients, and soliciting feedback throughout the contracting process. By listening attentively to client feedback and aligning solutions with their objectives, organizations can demonstrate their commitment to meeting and exceeding client expectations.

Delivering Value-Added Solutions

A customer-centric mindset emphasizes delivering value-added solutions that address client pain points, solve complex challenges, and drive meaningful outcomes. Organizations must focus on innovation, creativity, and continuous improvement to develop solutions that offer tangible benefits and add value to GSA contracting initiatives.

Delivering value-added solutions requires collaboration, agility, and a deep understanding of client requirements and industry best practices. Organizations must leverage their expertise, capabilities, and resources to design customized solutions that align with client goals and deliver measurable results.

Providing Exceptional Service and Support

Exceptional service and support are hallmarks of a customer-centric organization. Organizations must prioritize responsiveness, reliability, and accessibility in their interactions with GSA officials and clients, providing timely assistance and addressing concerns promptly throughout the contracting lifecycle.

Providing exceptional service involves maintaining open lines of communication, proactively addressing issues, and demonstrating a commitment to exceeding client expectations. Organizations must foster a culture of service excellence, empowering employees to go above and beyond to deliver exceptional experiences that build trust and loyalty with clients.

Anticipating Future Needs and Trends

A customer-centric mindset involves anticipating future needs and trends in the GSA marketplace to proactively address emerging challenges and capitalize on new opportunities. Organizations must stay abreast of industry trends, technological advancements, and regulatory changes that may impact client requirements and preferences.

Anticipating future needs requires strategic foresight, market intelligence, and a willingness to adapt to evolving client dynamics. Organizations must invest in continuous learning, research, and innovation to stay ahead of the curve and position themselves as trusted advisors and partners in meeting client needs.

Conclusion

Fostering a customer-centric mindset is essential for organizations seeking to build strong, enduring relationships and achieve success in GSA contracting. By understanding client needs, delivering value-added solutions, providing exceptional service and support, and anticipating future trends, organizations can differentiate themselves in the marketplace and become trusted partners in advancing client missions. In prioritizing a customer-centric approach, organizations demonstrate their commitment to excellence, innovation, and client satisfaction, laying the foundation for long-term success and growth in government contracting.

"The only thing that stands between you and your dream is the will to try and the belief that it is actually possible."
JOEL BROWN

Law 41

Invest in Talent Development and Retention: Invest in recruiting, training, and retaining top talent to build a skilled and motivated workforce capable of delivering exceptional performance on GSA contracts.

In the dynamic landscape of General Services Administration (GSA) contracting, investing in talent development and retention is paramount for organizations to build a skilled and motivated workforce capable of delivering exceptional performance. The success of GSA contracts hinges not only on technical expertise and capabilities but also on the dedication, creativity, and professionalism of employees. By prioritizing talent development and retention initiatives, organizations can foster a culture of excellence, drive innovation, and achieve sustainable growth in government contracting.

Identifying Skills and Competencies

The first step in talent development is identifying the skills, competencies, and capabilities required to excel in GSA contracting activities. Organizations must conduct thorough assessments of job roles, functions, and responsibilities to determine the critical skills and competencies needed to support GSA contracts effectively.

Identifying skills and competencies may involve conducting skills gap analyses, competency assessments, and performance evaluations to understand current capabilities and areas for improvement. By identifying key skills and competencies, organizations can align talent development initiatives with strategic objectives and business priorities.

Providing Training and Development Opportunities

Once skills and competencies are identified, organizations must provide training and development opportunities to enhance employee capabilities and performance. Training programs may encompass a range of topics, including GSA regulations, contract management best practices, negotiation skills, and compliance requirements.

Organizations should offer both technical and soft skills training tailored to the needs of employees involved in GSA contracting activities. Training programs may include classroom sessions, online courses, workshops, and seminars, supplemented by on-the-job training and mentorship opportunities.

Promoting Continuous Learning and Growth

Continuous learning and growth are fundamental principles of talent development in GSA contracting. Organizations must promote a culture of continuous learning, encouraging employees to seek out new knowledge, acquire new skills, and stay abreast of industry trends and best practices.

Promoting continuous learning involves providing access to learning resources, encouraging participation in professional development activities, and recognizing and rewarding employees for their commitment to personal and professional growth. Organizations should create opportunities for employees to apply their learning and contribute to organizational success through challenging assignments and cross-functional projects.

Fostering a Culture of Collaboration and Innovation

Talent development is not just about individual growth but also about fostering a culture of collaboration and innovation within the organization. Organizations must create an environment where employees feel empowered to share ideas, collaborate across teams, and experiment with new approaches to GSA contracting.

Fostering a culture of collaboration and innovation involves promoting open communication, recognizing and celebrating achievements, and providing opportunities for employees to contribute to process improvement initiatives and innovation projects. By fostering a culture of collaboration and innovation, organizations can harness the collective talents and creativity of their workforce to drive excellence in GSA contracting.

Conclusion

Investing in talent development and retention is a strategic imperative for organizations seeking to excel in GSA contracting. By identifying skills and competencies, providing training and development opportunities, promoting continuous learning and growth, and fostering a culture of collaboration and innovation, organizations can build a high-performing workforce capable of delivering exceptional results. In prioritizing talent development and retention, organizations demonstrate their commitment to employee success, organizational excellence, and long-term success in government contracting.

"Growth is the garden where
dreams take root; tend it with
diligence."
UNKNOWN

Law 42

Pursue Strategic Growth Opportunities: Identify and pursue strategic growth opportunities, such as expanding into new GSA Schedule categories or target markets, to diversify revenue streams and mitigate risk.

In the realm of General Services Administration (GSA) contracting, pursuing strategic growth opportunities is essential for organizations to expand their market presence, diversify revenue streams, and capitalize on emerging trends. Strategic growth opportunities encompass initiatives aimed at expanding into new GSA Schedule categories, target markets, geographic regions, or industry segments. By proactively pursuing strategic growth opportunities, organizations can position themselves for long-term success and resilience in the competitive landscape of government contracting.

Market Research and Analysis

The first step in pursuing strategic growth opportunities is conducting comprehensive market research and analysis to identify potential areas for expansion. Organizations must assess market trends, customer needs, competitive dynamics, and regulatory developments to pinpoint attractive growth opportunities within the GSA marketplace.

Market research may involve analyzing market size and growth projections, evaluating competitor strategies, and identifying gaps or unmet needs in existing offerings. By gaining a deep understanding of market dynamics, organizations can prioritize strategic growth opportunities that align with their strengths, capabilities, and long-term objectives.

Assessment of Organizational Capabilities

Before pursuing strategic growth opportunities, organizations must assess their internal capabilities, resources, and readiness to enter new markets or expand existing operations. This involves evaluating factors such as financial strength, technical expertise, workforce capacity, and operational scalability to determine the organization's ability to execute growth initiatives successfully.

Organizations must identify potential gaps or limitations in their capabilities and develop strategies to address them proactively. This may involve investing in talent development, acquiring new technologies, forming strategic partnerships, or restructuring internal processes to support growth objectives effectively.

Development of Market Entry Strategies

Once potential growth opportunities are identified and organizational capabilities assessed, organizations must develop market entry strategies tailored to each target market or segment. Market entry strategies may vary based on factors such as market maturity, competitive landscape, regulatory environment, and customer preferences.

Market entry strategies may include organic growth initiatives such as product development, geographic expansion, or market penetration strategies. Alternatively, organizations may explore inorganic growth opportunities through mergers, acquisitions, strategic alliances, or joint ventures to accelerate market entry and mitigate risks.

Execution and Implementation

Execution and implementation are critical phases in realizing strategic growth opportunities in GSA contracting. Organizations must develop clear action plans, set measurable objectives, and allocate resources effectively to execute growth initiatives successfully.

Effective execution requires strong leadership, cross-functional collaboration, and a disciplined approach to project management. Organizations must monitor progress closely, track key performance indicators, and adapt strategies based on market feedback and changing dynamics to ensure successful implementation of growth initiatives.

Evaluation and Continuous Improvement

After implementing growth initiatives, organizations must evaluate performance, analyze outcomes, and identify lessons learned to inform future growth strategies. Evaluation involves assessing the effectiveness of market entry strategies, measuring return on investment, and soliciting feedback from stakeholders to identify areas for improvement.

Continuous improvement is essential for organizations seeking sustainable growth in GSA contracting. Organizations must foster a culture of innovation, agility, and adaptability, encouraging employees to experiment, learn from failures, and iterate on strategies to drive continuous improvement and long-term success.

Conclusion

Pursuing strategic growth opportunities is essential for organizations seeking to thrive and succeed in the competitive landscape of GSA contracting. By conducting market research, assessing organizational capabilities, developing market entry strategies, executing initiatives effectively, and evaluating outcomes, organizations can position themselves for sustainable growth and resilience in government contracting. In prioritizing strategic growth, organizations demonstrate their commitment to innovation, adaptability, and long-term success in the dynamic landscape of GSA contracting.

"The way to get started is to
quit talking and begin doing."
WALT DISNEY

Law 43

**Leverage Technology for Competitive Advantage: Embrace
technology and innovation to gain a competitive edge in delivering innovative solutions and enhancing operational efficiency in fulfilling GSA contracts.**

In the modern landscape of General Services Administration
(GSA) contracting, leveraging technology is instrumental for organizations to gain a competitive edge, enhance operational efficiency, and deliver innovative solutions to clients. Technology
serves as a catalyst for transformation, enabling organizations to
streamline processes, optimize resource allocation, and adapt to
evolving market dynamics effectively. By embracing technology,
organizations can position themselves as industry leaders and
drive sustainable growth in the competitive GSA marketplace.

Identifying Technology Needs and Opportunities

The first step in leveraging technology for competitive advantage
is identifying organizational needs and opportunities for technological innovation. Organizations must conduct comprehensive
assessments of existing processes, workflows, and systems to
identify areas where technology can drive efficiency gains, improve decision-making, and enhance customer experiences.

Identifying technology needs may involve evaluating core business functions such as contract management, procurement, project management, and client engagement. Organizations must
also stay abreast of technological trends and emerging

innovations in the GSA marketplace to capitalize on new opportunities for differentiation and growth.

Investing in Technology Infrastructure and Solutions

Once technology needs are identified, organizations must invest in the development and implementation of technology infrastructure and solutions to support their strategic objectives. This may involve upgrading legacy systems, adopting cloud-based platforms, implementing enterprise resource planning (ERP) systems, or deploying specialized software solutions tailored to GSA contracting requirements.

Investing in technology infrastructure and solutions requires careful planning, resource allocation, and stakeholder buy-in. Organizations must prioritize investments that align with their long-term goals, deliver measurable benefits, and enhance the overall competitiveness and agility of the organization in the GSA marketplace.

Harnessing Data Analytics and Business Intelligence

Data analytics and business intelligence (BI) tools are powerful assets for organizations seeking to extract actionable insights, optimize decision-making, and drive performance improvements in GSA contracting activities. Organizations must harness data analytics and BI tools to analyze large datasets, identify trends, and make data-driven decisions that enhance efficiency and effectiveness.

Data analytics and BI enable organizations to monitor key performance indicators, track project progress, and identify areas for improvement in GSA contracting operations. By leveraging data analytics, organizations can optimize resource allocation, mitigate risks, and identify opportunities for innovation and growth in the GSA marketplace.

Embracing Digital Transformation

Digital transformation is a fundamental driver of competitive advantage in GSA contracting, enabling organizations to digitize processes, automate workflows, and enhance collaboration across teams and stakeholders. Organizations must embrace digital transformation initiatives that streamline operations, reduce costs, and enhance customer experiences in the GSA contracting lifecycle.

Digital transformation initiatives may include implementing electronic document management systems, digitizing procurement processes, and deploying collaboration tools to facilitate communication and knowledge sharing. By embracing digital transformation, organizations can position themselves as agile, customer-centric, and innovative partners in the GSA marketplace.

Fostering a Culture of Innovation and Agility

Leveraging technology for competitive advantage requires fostering a culture of innovation, agility, and continuous improvement within the organization. Organizations must empower employees to embrace technology, experiment with new tools and methodologies, and champion innovative solutions that drive value and differentiation in GSA contracting activities.

Fostering a culture of innovation and agility involves encouraging cross-functional collaboration, rewarding creativity and initiative, and providing opportunities for professional development and growth. By fostering a culture of innovation, organizations can harness the collective talents and creativity of their workforce to drive technological advancements and maintain a competitive edge in the GSA marketplace.

Conclusion

Leveraging technology for competitive advantage is essential for organizations seeking to thrive and succeed in the dynamic landscape of GSA contracting. By identifying technology needs and opportunities, investing in technology infrastructure and solutions, harnessing data analytics and business intelligence, embracing digital transformation, and fostering a culture of innovation and agility, organizations can position themselves as industry leaders and drive sustainable growth in government contracting. In prioritizing technology as a strategic enabler, organizations demonstrate their commitment to excellence, innovation, and long-term success in the competitive GSA marketplace.

"Coming together is a beginning, staying together is progress, and working together is success."
HENRY FORD

Law 44

Foster Cross-Functional Collaboration: Foster collaboration and synergy across departments, teams, and stakeholders within your organization to optimize coordination and execution of GSA contract requirements.

In the intricate world of General Services Administration (GSA) contracting, fostering cross-functional collaboration is essential for organizations to optimize coordination, enhance communication, and drive synergy across departments, teams, and stakeholders. GSA contracts often involve multifaceted requirements that demand collaboration among diverse functional areas such as business development, legal, finance, operations, and project management. By fostering cross-functional collaboration, organizations can leverage collective expertise, accelerate decision-making, and deliver superior outcomes in GSA contracting activities.

Breaking Down Silos and Barriers

The first step in fostering cross-functional collaboration is breaking down silos and barriers that impede communication and coordination across departments and teams. Organizations must cultivate an organizational culture that values transparency, inclusivity, and collaboration, encouraging employees to share information, seek input from diverse perspectives, and work together towards common goals.

Breaking down silos may involve restructuring organizational hierarchies, redefining roles and responsibilities, and implementing collaborative technologies and tools that facilitate communication and knowledge sharing across functional boundaries. By eliminating silos, organizations can foster a culture of teamwork and alignment, enabling cross-functional teams to collaborate effectively in pursuit of GSA contracting objectives.

Establishing Clear Goals and Objectives

Effective cross-functional collaboration requires establishing clear goals, objectives, and performance metrics that align with organizational priorities and GSA contracting requirements. Organizations must communicate strategic objectives and expectations clearly to all stakeholders, ensuring alignment and commitment to shared goals and outcomes.

Establishing clear goals and objectives fosters accountability, transparency, and alignment across functional areas, empowering employees to understand their roles and contributions towards achieving organizational success in GSA contracting activities. By setting clear expectations, organizations can minimize misunderstandings, conflicts, and inefficiencies that may arise from ambiguity or lack of alignment.

Promoting Open Communication and Knowledge Sharing

Open communication and knowledge sharing are foundational elements of effective cross-functional collaboration. Organizations must create opportunities for employees to exchange ideas, share best practices, and collaborate on GSA contracting initiatives through regular meetings, brainstorming sessions, and cross-functional workshops.

Promoting open communication involves creating a supportive and inclusive environment where employees feel empowered to voice their opinions, ask questions, and contribute insights without fear of judgment or reprisal. Organizations must leverage collaborative technologies such as project management tools, video conferencing platforms, and enterprise social networks to facilitate real-time communication and collaboration across geographically dispersed teams.

Encouraging Empathy and Respect

Empathy and respect are fundamental values that underpin successful cross-functional collaboration. Organizations must foster a culture of empathy and respect, encouraging employees to understand and appreciate the perspectives, expertise, and contributions of colleagues from diverse functional backgrounds.

Encouraging empathy and respect involves promoting active listening, empathy training, and conflict resolution skills to enhance interpersonal relationships and foster mutual understanding among team members. By fostering a culture of empathy and respect, organizations can create a supportive and inclusive work environment where diverse perspectives are valued, and collaborative relationships thrive.

Celebrating Success and Learning from Failure

Celebrating success and learning from failure are essential aspects of fostering cross-functional collaboration. Organizations must recognize and celebrate achievements, milestones, and contributions of cross-functional teams in achieving GSA contracting objectives, reinforcing a culture of collaboration and teamwork.

At the same time, organizations must embrace failure as an opportunity for learning and improvement, encouraging teams to reflect on challenges, identify root causes, and develop actionable insights for future collaboration. By celebrating success and learning from failure, organizations can foster a culture of continuous improvement and innovation in GSA contracting activities.

Conclusion

Fostering cross-functional collaboration is essential for organizations seeking to excel in the complex and dynamic landscape of GSA contracting. By breaking down silos, establishing clear goals and objectives, promoting open communication and knowledge sharing, encouraging empathy and respect, and celebrating success while learning from failure, organizations can leverage collective expertise and drive superior outcomes in GSA contracting activities. In prioritizing cross-functional collaboration, organizations demonstrate their commitment to excellence, teamwork, and organizational success in the competitive GSA marketplace.

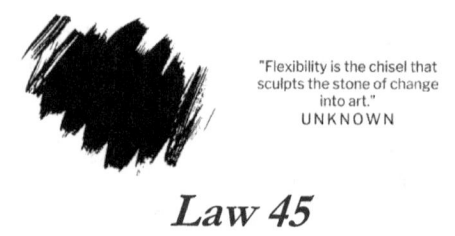

"Flexibility is the chisel that sculpts the stone of change into art."
UNKNOWN

Law 45

Cultivate Flexibility and Adaptability: Cultivate a culture of flexibility and adaptability to respond swiftly and effectively to changing requirements, priorities, and opportunities within GSA contracts and the broader marketplace.

In the ever-evolving terrain of General Services Administration (GSA) contracting, cultivating flexibility and adaptability is paramount for organizations to respond swiftly and effectively to changing requirements, priorities, and opportunities. GSA contracts are subject to dynamic market forces, regulatory changes, and shifting client needs, necessitating a proactive and agile approach to contracting activities. By embracing flexibility and adaptability, organizations can navigate uncertainties, capitalize on emerging trends, and sustain competitive advantage in the dynamic landscape of government contracting.

Embracing Change as a Constant

The cornerstone of cultivating flexibility and adaptability is embracing change as a constant in the GSA contracting landscape. Organizations must recognize that change is inevitable and pervasive, and that the ability to adapt to change is essential for survival and growth in the competitive marketplace.

Embracing change involves fostering a culture of openness, resilience, and curiosity, where employees are encouraged to embrace new ideas, challenge the status quo, and adapt to evolving circumstances proactively. By embracing change as a constant, organizations can foster a mindset of continuous improvement and innovation in GSA contracting activities.

Staying Nimble and Responsive

Staying nimble and responsive is essential for organizations seeking to cultivate flexibility and adaptability in GSA contracting. Organizations must prioritize agility and responsiveness in decision-making, resource allocation, and project execution to address changing requirements and client expectations effectively.

Staying nimble requires streamlining processes, reducing bureaucratic barriers, and empowering employees to make informed decisions and take decisive actions in response to changing circumstances. By staying nimble and responsive, organizations can capitalize on opportunities, mitigate risks, and maintain a competitive edge in the fast-paced environment of government contracting.

Anticipating and Managing Uncertainties

Anticipating and managing uncertainties is a critical aspect of cultivating flexibility and adaptability in GSA contracting. Organizations must develop robust risk management strategies, scenario planning techniques, and contingency plans to anticipate and mitigate potential disruptions and uncertainties in contracting activities.

Anticipating uncertainties involves conducting thorough risk assessments, analyzing potential impacts, and developing response strategies to address identified risks effectively. Organizations must remain vigilant, proactive, and resilient in managing uncertainties, leveraging cross-functional expertise and external insights to inform decision-making and risk mitigation efforts.

Fostering Learning and Innovation

Fostering a culture of learning and innovation is essential for organizations to cultivate flexibility and adaptability in GSA contracting. Organizations must encourage experimentation, creativity, and continuous improvement, empowering employees to explore new ideas, technologies, and approaches to contracting activities.

Fostering learning and innovation involves providing opportunities for professional development, knowledge sharing, and cross-functional collaboration to stimulate creativity and problem-solving. Organizations must celebrate successes, learn from failures, and institutionalize best practices to drive a culture of continuous learning and innovation in GSA contracting activities.

Embracing Change as an Opportunity

Above all, cultivating flexibility and adaptability requires organizations to embrace change as an opportunity for growth and transformation. Organizations must view change as a catalyst for innovation, improvement, and reinvention, rather than a barrier to progress or stability.

Embracing change as an opportunity involves reframing challenges as learning experiences, embracing ambiguity, and embracing experimentation and iteration in pursuit of excellence. By embracing change as an opportunity, organizations can foster resilience, agility, and adaptability in GSA contracting activities, positioning themselves for long-term success and sustainability in the competitive marketplace.

Conclusion

Cultivating flexibility and adaptability is essential for organizations seeking to thrive and succeed in the dynamic landscape of General Services Administration (GSA) contracting. By embracing change as a constant, staying nimble and responsive, anticipating and managing uncertainties, fostering learning and innovation, and embracing change as an opportunity, organizations can navigate uncertainties, capitalize on opportunities, and sustain competitive advantage in the fast-paced environment of government contracting. In prioritizing flexibility and adaptability, organizations demonstrate their commitment to resilience, agility, and organizational success in the competitive GSA marketplace.

"The future depends on what you do today."
MAHATMA GANDHI

Law 46

Demonstrate Commitment to Sustainability and Social Responsibility: Integrate sustainability and social responsibility initiatives into your business practices and GSA contract

deliverables to align with evolving client expectations and regulatory trends.

In the conscientious realm of General Services Administration (GSA) contracting, demonstrating commitment to sustainability and social responsibility is not only a moral imperative but also a strategic advantage. GSA contracts increasingly prioritize environmental sustainability, diversity, equity, inclusion, and ethical business practices. By embracing sustainability and social responsibility, organizations can align with client expectations, mitigate risks, and enhance their reputation in the competitive landscape of government contracting.

Embracing Environmental Sustainability

Embracing environmental sustainability involves adopting practices that minimize environmental impact, conserve natural resources, and promote eco-friendly solutions in GSA contracting activities. Organizations must integrate principles of sustainability into their operations, supply chain management, and product/service offerings to support environmental stewardship and climate resilience.

Embracing environmental sustainability may involve initiatives such as reducing carbon emissions, minimizing waste generation, optimizing energy efficiency, and sourcing renewable materials. By embracing environmental sustainability, organizations can contribute to global efforts to address climate change, while also reducing operational costs and enhancing brand reputation.

Promoting Diversity, Equity, and Inclusion (DEI)

Promoting diversity, equity, and inclusion (DEI) is essential for organizations to foster a culture of belonging, respect, and equal opportunity in GSA contracting activities. Organizations must prioritize diversity and inclusivity in recruitment, hiring, promotion, and supplier diversity initiatives to create a workforce and supply chain that reflects the diversity of society.

Promoting DEI involves implementing policies and practices that eliminate bias, discrimination, and barriers to advancement based on race, ethnicity, gender, age, sexual orientation, disability, and other protected characteristics. By promoting diversity, equity, and inclusion, organizations can tap into diverse perspectives, talents, and experiences, driving innovation, creativity, and performance excellence in GSA contracting.

Adhering to Ethical Business Practices

Adhering to ethical business practices is fundamental for organizations to uphold integrity, trust, and transparency in GSA contracting activities. Organizations must operate with honesty, fairness, and accountability in all dealings with clients, suppliers, employees, and other stakeholders, adhering to legal and regulatory requirements and industry standards.

Adhering to ethical business practices involves maintaining high standards of integrity, avoiding conflicts of interest, and ensuring transparency in decision-making and financial reporting. Organizations must cultivate a culture of ethical conduct, providing employees with training, guidance, and resources to navigate ethical dilemmas and make principled decisions in GSA contracting activities.

Engaging in Community Engagement and Philanthropy

Engaging in community engagement and philanthropy is integral for organizations to contribute positively to society and address pressing social challenges in GSA contracting activities. Organizations must invest in programs and initiatives that support local communities, promote education, healthcare, and economic development, and address social and environmental issues.

Engaging in community engagement and philanthropy may involve volunteering, charitable giving, corporate social responsibility (CSR) initiatives, and partnerships with non-profit organizations and community stakeholders. By engaging in community engagement and philanthropy, organizations can build meaningful relationships, enhance brand reputation, and create shared value for stakeholders in GSA contracting activities.

Conclusion

Demonstrating commitment to sustainability and social responsibility is essential for organizations seeking to thrive and succeed in the competitive landscape of General Services Administration (GSA) contracting. By embracing environmental sustainability, promoting diversity, equity, and inclusion, adhering to ethical business practices, and engaging in community engagement and philanthropy, organizations can align with client expectations, mitigate risks, and enhance their reputation as responsible corporate citizens. In prioritizing sustainability and social responsibility, organizations demonstrate their commitment to ethical conduct, stakeholder engagement, and long-term success in the competitive GSA marketplace.

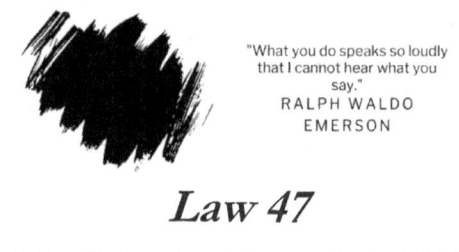

"What you do speaks so loudly that I cannot hear what you say."
RALPH WALDO EMERSON

Law 47

Manage Stakeholder Expectations Effectively: Proactively manage stakeholder expectations, including those of GSA officials, clients, subcontractors, and employees, to foster alignment, minimize misunderstandings, and enhance collaboration.

Effectively managing stakeholder expectations is essential for organizations engaged in General Services Administration (GSA) contracting to foster alignment, minimize misunderstandings, and enhance collaboration throughout the contract lifecycle. Stakeholders in GSA contracting activities may include GSA officials, clients, subcontractors, employees, and other key partners involved in the contract execution process. By proactively managing stakeholder expectations, organizations can build trust, mitigate risks, and drive successful outcomes in GSA contracting endeavors.

Identifying Key Stakeholders

The first step in managing stakeholder expectations effectively is identifying key stakeholders who have a vested interest or influence in the GSA contracting process. Stakeholders may include GSA contracting officers, project managers, client representatives, subcontractors, legal counsel, finance personnel, and internal team members responsible for contract execution.

Identifying key stakeholders involves conducting stakeholder analysis to map out their roles, interests, concerns, and expectations related to GSA contracts. By understanding the perspectives and priorities of key stakeholders, organizations can tailor communication and engagement strategies to address their needs effectively.

Establishing Clear Communication Channels

Establishing clear communication channels is essential for facilitating dialogue, sharing information, and managing expectations among stakeholders in GSA contracting activities. Organizations must establish formal and informal communication channels that enable stakeholders to stay informed, provide feedback, and address concerns throughout the contract lifecycle.

Clear communication channels may include regular meetings, status reports, email updates, project management tools, and collaborative platforms for sharing documents and information. Organizations must ensure that communication channels are accessible, transparent, and responsive to the needs of diverse stakeholders involved in GSA contracting activities.

Setting Realistic Expectations

Setting realistic expectations is crucial for managing stakeholder perceptions and fostering trust in GSA contracting endeavors. Organizations must establish clear, achievable objectives, milestones, and deliverables that align with stakeholder needs, project requirements, and contractual obligations.

Setting realistic expectations involves conducting thorough scoping and planning exercises to define project scope, timelines, resource requirements, and performance metrics upfront. Organizations must communicate expectations openly, manage scope creep effectively, and address any discrepancies or changes in stakeholder expectations proactively to avoid misunderstandings and conflicts during contract execution.

Providing Timely Updates and Progress Reports

Providing timely updates and progress reports is essential for keeping stakeholders informed about the status, progress, and performance of GSA contracts. Organizations must establish regular reporting cadences and milestones to communicate key achievements, milestones, risks, and issues encountered throughout the contract lifecycle.

Timely updates and progress reports may include status meetings, written reports, dashboards, and presentations that highlight project progress, achievements, challenges, and mitigation strategies. Organizations must ensure that progress reports are clear, concise, and actionable, providing stakeholders with the information they need to make informed decisions and take appropriate actions in GSA contracting activities.

Managing Change and Resolving Conflicts

Managing change and resolving conflicts are inevitable aspects of GSA contracting that require proactive engagement and collaboration among stakeholders. Organizations must establish change management processes and conflict resolution mechanisms to address changes in project scope, requirements, priorities, and disputes that may arise during contract execution.

Managing change involves assessing impacts, evaluating alternatives, and obtaining stakeholder buy-in before implementing changes to project scope, timelines, or deliverables. Similarly, resolving conflicts requires open dialogue, active listening, and negotiation skills to find mutually acceptable resolutions that preserve relationships and project objectives in GSA contracting activities.

Conclusion

Effective management of stakeholder expectations is essential for organizations seeking to drive successful outcomes in General Services Administration (GSA) contracting. By identifying key stakeholders, establishing clear communication channels, setting realistic expectations, providing timely updates and progress reports, and managing change and resolving conflicts proactively, organizations can foster alignment, trust, and collaboration throughout the contract lifecycle. In prioritizing stakeholder management, organizations demonstrate their commitment to transparency, accountability, and stakeholder engagement in the competitive landscape of GSA contracting.

"We are what we repeatedly do. Excellence, then, is not an act but a habit."
ARISTOTLE

Law 48

Reflect, Learn, and Iterate: Foster a culture of reflection, continuous learning, and iteration to glean insights from past experiences, successes, and failures in GSA contracting and drive ongoing improvement and innovation.

In the intricate landscape of General Services Administration (GSA) contracting, the ability to reflect, learn, and iterate is indispensable for organizations to glean insights from past experiences, successes, and failures, and drive ongoing improvement and innovation in their contracting endeavors. Reflecting on past performance, learning from lessons learned, and iterating on processes and strategies enable organizations to adapt to evolving requirements, optimize performance, and enhance competitiveness in the dynamic GSA marketplace.

The Power of Reflection

Reflection is a powerful tool for organizations engaged in GSA contracting to assess their performance, identify areas for improvement, and celebrate achievements. Organizations must create opportunities for individuals and teams involved in contracting activities to reflect on their experiences, challenges, and successes throughout the contract lifecycle.

Reflection involves asking critical questions, soliciting feedback from stakeholders, and analyzing data and performance metrics to understand what worked well and what could be improved in GSA contracting endeavors. By fostering a culture of reflection, organizations can cultivate a mindset of continuous improvement and learning that drives excellence and innovation in contracting activities.

Learning from Experience

Learning from experience is essential for organizations to extract valuable insights and lessons learned from past GSA contracting endeavors. Organizations must capture, document, and disseminate knowledge and best practices gained from previous contracts to inform decision-making, mitigate risks, and enhance performance in future contracting activities.

Learning from experience involves conducting post-mortem reviews, debriefings, and after-action reports to analyze project outcomes, identify root causes of successes and failures, and develop actionable recommendations for improvement. By institutionalizing a culture of learning from experience, organizations can build institutional knowledge and resilience that enables them to navigate uncertainties and challenges effectively in GSA contracting.

Iterating for Continuous Improvement

Iteration is the process of refining, optimizing, and evolving processes, strategies, and approaches based on insights and feedback gathered from reflection and learning. Organizations must embrace iteration as a fundamental principle of continuous improvement in GSA contracting activities, seeking opportunities to refine and enhance their practices over time.

Iterating for continuous improvement involves implementing changes, experimenting with new ideas, and testing hypotheses to address identified gaps and opportunities in contracting processes and strategies. Organizations must foster a culture of experimentation, agility, and adaptability that encourages individuals and teams to innovate and iterate on their approaches to GSA contracting.

Embracing Innovation

Embracing innovation is essential for organizations to stay ahead of the curve and drive meaningful change in the GSA marketplace. Organizations must encourage creativity, experimentation, and disruptive thinking to challenge the status quo and identify new opportunities for innovation and value creation in contracting activities.

Embracing innovation involves investing in research and development, fostering cross-functional collaboration, and embracing emerging technologies and methodologies that have the potential to transform GSA contracting practices. By embracing innovation, organizations can differentiate themselves from competitors, unlock new sources of value, and drive sustainable growth and success in the competitive GSA marketplace.

Conclusion

Reflecting, learning, and iterating are essential components of success for organizations engaged in General Services Administration (GSA) contracting. By harnessing the power of reflection to assess performance, learning from experience to extract valuable insights, iterating for continuous improvement, and embracing innovation to drive meaningful change, organizations can adapt to evolving requirements, optimize performance, and enhance competitiveness in the dynamic GSA marketplace. In prioritizing reflection, learning, and iteration, organizations demonstrate their commitment to excellence, innovation, and continuous improvement in the competitive landscape of GSA contracting.

The 48 Laws of GSA Contracting Conclusion:

The journey through the intricate landscape of General Services Administration (GSA) contracting, as explored across the diverse chapters from 1 through 48, unveils a comprehensive roadmap for success in this dynamic arena. Each chapter delves into essential principles, strategies, and insights that collectively shape the fabric of effective engagement, management, and optimization within the realm of GSA contracts.

From the foundational principles of choosing battles wisely and understanding market dynamics to the intricate nuances of fostering cross-functional collaboration and managing stakeholder expectations, the chapters offer a holistic perspective on navigating the multifaceted challenges and opportunities inherent in GSA contracting.

At its core, GSA contracting demands a blend of strategic foresight, operational excellence, ethical conduct, and adaptability to thrive amidst evolving regulations, market dynamics, and stakeholder expectations. It necessitates a commitment to transparency, integrity, and innovation, underpinned by a relentless pursuit of excellence and continuous improvement.

The chapters underscore the importance of cultivating strong relationships, embracing change, harnessing the power of data and analytics, and staying attuned to emerging trends and regulatory shifts. They emphasize the imperative of delivering exceptional value, protecting reputation, and fostering a culture of excellence and social responsibility to succeed in the competitive GSA marketplace.

Moreover, they highlight the significance of reflection, learning, and iteration as catalysts for growth, innovation, and resilience in GSA contracting endeavors. By embracing these principles and integrating them into their organizational DNA, entities engaged in GSA contracting can forge a path toward sustainable success, propelled by a commitment to integrity, collaboration, and customer-centricity.

As organizations embark on their GSA contracting journey, they are reminded that success is not merely a destination, but a continual journey marked by adaptability, innovation, and a steadfast dedication to excellence. With the insights gleaned from these chapters as guiding beacons, organizations can navigate the complexities of GSA contracting with confidence, purpose, and a relentless pursuit of excellence.